I0154459

ECHOES

FROM HEAVEN

Topical Study Devotions
That Reveal the God Who Speaks

The voice of the Lord is over the waters; the God of glory thunders; the Lord thunders over the mighty waters. The voice of the Lord is powerful; the voice of the Lord is majestic. The voice of the Lord breaks the cedars; the Lord breaks in pieces the cedars of Lebanon. He makes Lebanon skip like a calf, Sirion like a young wild ox. The voice of the Lord strikes with flashes of lightning. The voice of the Lord shakes the desert; the Lord shakes the Desert of Kadesh. The voice of the Lord twists the oaks and strips the forests bare. Psalm 29:3-9a

And a voice from heaven said, "This is my Son, whom I love; with him I am well pleased." Matthew 3:17

www.echoesfromheaven.org

Echoes From Heaven
2nd Edition

Lauralee
©COPYRIGHT 2020

Scripture taken from the HOLY BIBLE, NEW INTERNATIONAL VERSION, copyright 1973, 1978, 1984, by International Bible Society, Inc. Used by permission of Zondervan. All rights reserved worldwide.

Scripture quotations from the KJV are from the King James Version and are in the public domain.

Scripture quotations marked ESV are from the ESV Bible (The Holy Bible, English Standard Version), copyright 2001 by Crossway Bible, a publishing ministry of Good News Publishers. ESV Text Edition 2007. Used by permission. All rights reserved.

Scripture quotations marked HCSB, are taken from the Holman Christian Standard Bible, Copyright 1999, 2000, 2002, 2003, 2009, by Holman Bible Publishers. Used by permission. HCSB is a federally registered trademark of Holman Bible Publishers.

Holy Bible, New Living Translation, copyright 1996, 2004, 2015 by Tyndale House Foundation. Used by permission of Tyndale House Publishers Inc., Carol Stream, Illinois 60188. All rights reserved.

No part of this publication, *Echoes From Heaven*, may be reproduced, stored in a retrieval system, or transmitted in any form or by any means without prior written permission of the author. I prefer that this book not be resold, but it may freely be given away as a gift, or passed along freely to another, in order to bless someone.

Published by Lauralee Dunfee Swarbrick, June, 2020

www.echoesfromheaven.org

Cover By: Gabriel Valles

Education Matters Press

ISBN 978-1-939064-85-1

Dedicated To All Those Adopted or In Foster Care Who Through No Fault of Their Own Struggle With Loss

Especially To All Those Who Have Attended Skiin' With The Galilean Bible Camp

With heartfelt love to those Dearest Ones:

David,
David Jr. & Kathleen, Matthew & Leigh Anne
Eric, Will
Caroline, Annabeth, Ariel

Special Thanks For Prayer Ministers
Elizabeth Gealy Castiglioni
Patti Freeman Nelson
Liz Weinert

Special Honor to David Swarbrick, Jr. Partner in Ministry
David Provides Creative Insight
Dynamic Vision, & Excels in Zeal for the Lord

Special Thanks to Cindy Holladay Montgomery and Lisa Holladay Sepulveda
Highly Favored Women
Acknowledgment of Gracious Assistance From Sandra Gaiser
With Double Honor To All Of God's Soldiers of The Cross

To God Be The Glory

Dear Reader,

When I was a teenager I was in a dark place and disappointment shrouded me. I couldn't find the way. My brother was killed in a car accident when I was fifteen and it broke my heart. I found myself yelling at a God I didn't know. I started reading the Bible and as I read, I became very attracted to this Jesus, who responded masterfully even when people let him down. In my heart I desired to be like Him. I was still angry at God, for allowing my brother to be taken from me and couldn't accept God's Jesus until I read Romans 8:28 and learned all things work together for good to those who love God and are called according to his purposes. God in his upside down kindness was giving me a severe mercy and using it to lead me to a relationship, a friendship. This friendship with the God of the universe would come at a price. The cost was that people close to me didn't seem to understand the value of the treasure that I just unearthed.

Life continued on and I held onto this treasured relationship with God the Father through Jesus the Son and empowered by God the Spirit. As I held onto the treasure, I also held onto a backpack of burdens. I was stuck. I had repetitive cycles of broken relationships, and I wanted to be whole, I wanted to be able to move forward. I wanted close family and friends and I desperately wanted freedom, but somehow inextricably I pushed people away. I continued in isolation and loneliness. My greatest frustration was I wasn't who I wanted to be. I deeply desired to be a better wife, a better mother and a better friend, but I wasn't that person. I dealt with my broken personality through working long days and achieving my goals.

Initially I didn't know what was contained in the backpack I carried, but I did learn the contents over time. In many ways the contents of the backpack are unimportant, suffice it to say I had deep childhood wounds as a result of evil actions committed against me as a child, in addition to the sorrow from losing my brother. These evil actions coupled with my loss, resulted in a deep sense of feeling as though I didn't fit. I felt comfortable hiding underground. Although I was comfortable, I really wanted to come above ground and be fully myself and set free. I sought God to bring me out of the dark hole I was in.

Over the course of many years I have come above ground and gotten rid of my backpack. It no longer is attached to me. I have obtained freedom and I now live confidently. In these pages are treasures of wisdom that have been mined over many years. These treasures of wisdom helped me to resolve my relationships and I am now in a place of peace. As you mine for treasures of wisdom, I give you this diamond-Jesus is trustworthy-He is precious. Resolution inherently meant life with pain and friendship, chosen over a dead heart and isolation. The heart struggles to be fleshy and alive rather than stony and dead. Life, knowing Him and having healthy close intimate family and friends along with internal freedom await those who mine carefully and steadily.

I hope these devotions will resonate with your heart. Wisdom moves miners to find jewels of freedom and friendship with God and with men. The beauty of truly, really knowing God is that you can find your heart and you can become sweet hearted or gallant hearted. Becoming the best you can be, confidently liking who you are is a beautiful place to be. You too can obtain this treasure. Jesus continues to set captives free today.

Lauralee

Table of Contents:

Sins of The Heart

Growing As a Disciple of Christ

Personal Growth And Development

God Is Creator

Understanding How God Fathers Us

> *In the beginning God created the heavens and the earth. Now the earth was formless and empty, darkness was over the surface of the deep, and the Spirit of God was hovering over the waters. Genesis 1:1-2*

So the majesty of God is that He created the world. On the first day that God created, He created light and He called the light day. On the next day, God created the sky. On the third day of creation, God created the land and the seas. On this same day God also created plants and vegetation. On the fourth day, God created the sun, the moon and the stars. On the fifth day, God created fish, sea animals, and birds. On the sixth day God created land animals and mankind. On the seventh day, God rested from His work. God is a god of rest and we should follow His example and incorporate deep rest into our lives. At the end of everything that God created, the Scriptures state that what God made was good. All that God created was good.

In the history of the creation of the world, Genesis 2 shows some of the particulars of what happened on the sixth day when God created mankind. During his creative work, God made a man and a woman out of the completed man Adam and He placed the couple in the Garden of Eden. The Garden of Eden is described as having a flowing river that separated into four headwaters-Pishon, Gihon, Tigris and Euphrates. The Garden of Eden is described as a plentiful garden where food-bearing trees grew. In addition to these trees there were also two other unique trees, the tree of life, and the tree of the knowledge of good and evil.

From the beginning, God ruled over man. God instructed man to not eat from the tree of the knowledge of good and evil, but the serpent deceived mankind, man fell, and man was banished from the Garden of Eden. God placed a cherubim and a flaming sword flashing back and forth to guard the way to the tree of life.

Our God is God and there is no other. The triune God-God the Father, God the Word, and God the Holy Spirit is the God of creation, everyone else besides God are created beings. God enjoys creating and because we are like Him, He enjoys seeing us create as well. God is so kind that He joys over us. He likes creativity. Like the joy of hearing water splashing, so our God enjoys seeing us create memories, and friendships, and art projects, and books, and buildings, and companies, and houses, and communities of faith that reflect His glory.

Further Study: Genesis 1, 2, 3; Hebrews 11:3

God Is A Covenantal God-Greater Than Indiana Jones
Understanding How God Fathers Us

When the sun had set and darkness had fallen, a smoking fire pot with a blazing torch appeared and passed between the pieces. Genesis 15:17

When we think of the Ark of the Covenant, many of us think of Indiana Jones. In the Raiders of the Lost Ark movie, we remember that the power of God came out of the Ark and Indiana had to shut his eyes and not look so that his life would be preserved and he would not die. The picture of Indiana, is reflective of 1 Samuel 6:19 where the Lord struck down seventy men for looking into the Ark. The Ark of the Covenant was a religious object that the Lord demanded must be treated with extreme respect. The words that came from God were carefully noted and kept within the Ark. The law of God and the Ten Commandments were contained in the Ark. In the Old Testament the bread was set out before the Lord, Sabbath after Sabbath on behalf of the Israelites as a lasting covenant. God set the priests up as care takers of the Ark and as the ones tasked with encouraging the people to follow the laws of God in the community. So the Ark of the Covenant was symbolic of the covenant of God, but it also contained the scrolls of God, holy words, that were life giving to the people of God, the Israelites.

God's original covenant with the Israelites is recorded in Genesis 15 and Genesis 17. These two chapters are two of the most fascinating chapters in the entire Bible. There are many other scriptures that record God restating his covenant to the Israelites throughout history. Additionally, men of God mimic God and make covenants, oaths, or promises among themselves throughout the Old Testament. In the Old Testament those who closely followed

12

God, gave their word carefully and with fidelity. Their word was as good as gold.

Within the Old Testament record, God is beautifully revealed as the God of Covenant. God in his greatness desires to know people closely. God beckons his people to be in relationship with Him. God is a consuming fire and filled with majesty. He is the God who draws His people into covenantal relationship. The word covenant means allegiance or pledge. God is so fascinating in that He has made a pledge to us, an allegiance to us. God has pledged His faithfulness to us, and wants us to pledge our faithfulness to Him. God, the God of Covenant, in fact has called us into a partnership of love with Him. This is indeed a truth that is beyond marvelous. The God of Covenant has made many promises of faithful love to us, His people.

Further Study: Genesis 6:18, 9:1-17, 15, 17, 31; Exodus 2:24, 19:5, 25:16, 31:16, 32:15, Leviticus 26:9, Numbers 1:50-53, 9:15, 10:17,18; Deuteronomy 7:9-12, 29:9; Joshua 4; 1Samuel 23:18; 1Kings 3:15; 2Kings 11; Psalm 25:4; Daniel 9:4, Malachi 2

God Is My Protector, My Shield
Understanding How God Fathers Us

> *Surely, Lord, you bless the righteous; you surround them with your favor as with a shield. Psalm 5:12*
>
> *The Lord is my rock, my fortress and my deliverer; my God is my rock, in whom I take refuge, my shield and the horn of my salvation, my stronghold. Psalm 18:2*

Some of us have been unshielded as children, and we come to faith in Christ either out of broken families who did not know the Lord or from families who were not obedient to the Lord's call on their lives. In both cases, we may have suffered from the ravages of sin and felt very unprotected due to abuse or neglect of various kinds. As we grow in faith in the Lord, we rest in the fact that God is our shield. In terms of warfare, a shield is protective equipment-it deflects arrows, swords and other attacks from the enemy. The need for a shield itself implies that there are and there will be attacks from the enemy. If you were wounded as a child, the evil one wants you to believe that your life is beyond repair-he wants you to despair, he wants you to be depressed, and he wants you to believe that God does not love you nor care for you.

Contrary to all of this, please believe and know that God loves you. The Lord in His kindness has provided for us the shield of faith. Every day remember that God exists and He is so kind that He will reward those who earnestly seek Him. Further, God provides us with protection. Our God is a refuge for us. A refuge is a place to hide out in safety from whatever pitfalls our life is presenting to us in the current challenges we face. More extravagantly, Scripture says the Lord blesses the righteous and surrounds them with favor. We are not to ask for favor friend, we are to thank God for favor. The Lord has kindly given us favor. It is indeed His shield upon us. If you are not feeling favored right now, it does not mean you are not favored. If you are in Christ, if you believe in Him and trust Jesus with your life, He is surrounding you with favor.

Further Study: Genesis 15:1, Deuteronomy 33:29, Proverbs 30:5, Zechariah 12:8, Hebrews 11

God Is My Deliverer, A Different Kind of Mailman
Understanding How God Fathers Us

> And lead us not into temptation, but deliver us from the evil one. Matthew 6:13 (Jesus)
>
> The Lord is my rock, my fortress and my deliverer. Psalm 18:2
>
> So I say, walk by the Spirit, and you will not gratify the desires of the flesh. Galatians 5:16

In the Lord's Prayer, Jesus shows us how to pray. Kindly, Jesus is patient and tenderhearted with us and tells us to specifically pray for deliverance. You won't be taught much about this at the school you are attending and you certainly won't hear it on any of the news stations. The truth is that the Lord God is our deliverer. What does it mean to be delivered? This is like welcome news that arrives in our mailbox from another state. The mailman delivers letters from one state to another state. In a similar way, when God delivers us, He moves us from one state of being to another state of being. Deliverance means then to be moved in some way from a state where one has a struggle to a state where that struggle is broken and new freedom is experienced. Throughout the ministry of Jesus, spiritual deliverance was experienced early in one's faith history when people encountered Jesus for the first time and were moved from the state of living without God to the state of living with God through an initial response of faith. These dramatic spiritual deliverances from one state to another state, resulted in a positional movement from the kingdom of darkness into the kingdom of light. Many times, people saw an undeniable change in the one who was delivered.

In addition to this, deliverance is also used repeatedly in the Old Testament to mean escape from one's enemies; enemies who oppose you by working against you sometimes with slander, or enemies who oppose you with seeking your physical death. Absalom set himself outside the city gates and slandered King David. The Philistines repeatedly attacked the Israelites. Then to be delivered would mean the silencing of Absalom or military victory over the Philistines. David moved from the state of being slandered by Absalom to Absalom being silenced, and the Israelites moved from the state of being physically attacked by the Philistines to the state of being physically victorious over the Philistines. The Lord delivered both King David and the Israelites.

The question remains, how does deliverance come? To be delivered, to be set free from sins' grip or set free from physical opposition requires the work of the Spirit of the Lord which most often comes with prayer and worship. You can expect to receive from God if you continue to place yourself in the streams where the Spirit flows. The move of the Spirit of the Lord does not only happen in church buildings, although for sure the Lord does work there. The movements of the Spirit of the Lord cannot be controlled, however the movements of the Spirit of the Lord occur where God is welcomed. When we welcome God into our lives by singing to the Lord, seeking the Lord, or praying to the Lord; then we are in a position to receive from the Lord. But the main thing is we must be praying to be guarded from the evil one. The Christian must continually move away from evil and follow after good.

We know there are evil deeds that are prominent in our culture and the truth is we are all susceptible to sin's snares and so we must pray that we would be delivered from the evil that has been planted in the garden of our hearts. The best way to deal with the evil is to get planting good ideas and good thoughts, meditating on God daily. Pray for deliverance, but plant new seeds of faith, hope, and love. Pray in the Spirit and plant God's word, God's songs, and encouragement from God's people in your hearts. Pray and plant. Before you know it, you will be delivered from evil and more good things will be growing in the garden of your heart.

Further Study: Psalm 1, Matthew 13, Matthew 20:1-16, Matthew 21:33-46

Special thanks to David Swarbrick, Jr.

God Provides Security
Hey, Turn Around & Stop Cycling
Understanding How God Fathers Us

Even though I walk through the darkest valley, I will fear no evil, for you are with me; your rod and your staff, they comfort me. Psalm 23:4

Dear friends, it is a difficult concept for an adolescent to understand that guidance is security. A child who grows up and does not receive guidance has difficulty finding their way. If you are receiving guidance, you are being loved. Think of it this way. If you want to go to California, do you want someone to tell you that you are on the road to New York five minutes after you've left home or ten hours after you've left home? Of course we'd all like to know right away if we are headed in the wrong direction. In the same way, welcome guidance so that you will know sooner rather than later when you've taken off in the wrong direction. God wants you to have guidance so that your path through life will be smoother. God, in his great kindness, wants to give you clear boundaries that keep you from cycling aimlessly through life (in endless cycles), getting lost, or getting hurt.

As a Christian, the Lord provides you with guidance through His Word and through His Holy Spirit. The Lord provides you with guidance through the gift of your parents or foster parents. The Lord also provides you with guidance through your conscience. The Lord provides you with guidance through the pastors and Bible study teachers at many of our great churches. All of these: the Bible, the Holy Spirit, your parents, your conscience, and your pastors and leaders at your church; serve to help guide you in your life. At every point of our lives all of us, no matter our age, are forever learners. This is what being a disciple means. We are forever a learner of the ways of Jesus. As a learner, we learn to correct our ways as we go.

God invites us to welcome correction because correction helps us to grow into becoming powerful future leaders. Truly great men and women of God welcome God's rod and staff and they find security and comfort in being guided and corrected. They find security and comfort that they won't be left on the road to New York when they want to go to California.

Further Study: Job 5:17, Proverbs 12:1, 13:24, Hebrews 12:1-13, Revelations 3:19

God Is Not Mute-God Speaks

Understanding How God Fathers Us

> *The Lord would speak to Moses face to face. Exodus 33:11*
>
> *In the past God spoke to our ancestors through the prophets at many times and in various ways, but in these last days He has spoken to us by his Son. Hebrews 1:1-2*
>
> *My sheep hear my voice, and I know them, and they follow me. John 10:27 (Jesus) (KJV)*

Throughout Scripture there are numerous accounts of God talking with people. One of the most dramatic examples of God talking was on Mount Sinai when God spoke to Moses in a burning bush. Another dramatic example was when God spoke to Abram and gave Him the covenant during his sleep. It is so wonderful to understand that God spoke in the past and He still speaks today. So many people when they are young in the Lord want to know what is the right thing to do. They want to hear from God and get exact directions about what they should do with their life. They want God to speak to them. The preponderance of evidence supports the belief that God speaks. But how does God speak, how does He do it?

God speaks in a myriad number of ways. First of all, God speaks to us through the Bible. The Bible shows us the mind of God and the Bible is active and alive and works to purify our attitudes and motives. The Bible is one of the primary ways God speaks to us. Secondly, God has spoken to us through creation. The world declares the glory of God and the power of God, far exceeding human capacity to create. Thirdly, God has now primarily spoken to us through his son Jesus. Jesus is God coming from heaven to show us how to live. Fourthly, God speaks to us through the Holy Spirit. When we receive Jesus by faith, then the Holy Spirit indwells us and we hear from Him. Fifthly we can hear from God by his speaking through the people of God. Sixthly, God speaks to us through our conscience. Our conscience either excuses or accuses us depending upon our choices and our motives. Finally, God can speak to us through His direct speech, and through special revelations including things like dreams and visions.

God speaks, He has a loud voice, but not everyone is paying attention. If you want to hear from God, then learn to be silent and attentive in His presence. Sit silently in creation, and search with diligence to hear from God. Everyone can hear from God daily from looking on creation, reading the word and praying, however, specific guidance from God requires pursuit and careful living.

Further Study: Psalm 29, Matthew 3:11, Lk 1:26-38, 3:2; John 14:26, John 20:22, Acts 9:5-19, 11:28, 18:9-10, 26:14-18; 1Corinthians 2:16; 2Timothy 3:16, Hebrews 1:1-3, 4:12

Special thanks to David Swarbrick, Jr. who created the saying, "God is not mute".

Pardon the Interruption; It's Me, God
Understanding How God Fathers Us

To those who sold doves he said, "Get these out of here! Stop turning my Father's house into a market!" John 2:16

Dear Friends, at some point we all receive correction. The way to think about this is to understand that God is God and we are not. Please don't be so hard on yourself if you have made a mistake. Try to understand that all of us make mistakes. It is not only teenagers that make mistakes. Adults also make mistakes. At points in all of our lives each one of us must look at what we are doing and make a decision to stop doing that thing or change our attitude about something. God is willing to interrupt us when we are doing the wrong thing. When I was a kid I always thought it was fun to mock people. After all, that is what the cool crowd did. But when I got to know Jesus, I turned my back on the mocking behavior. I want nothing to do with ever being a mocker. Yet still occasionally as an adult I laugh a bit at others.

I was making a joke about my husband playing bumper cars...he twice backed into other people. I thought the whole bumper car thing was cute and funny. But I was letting him be the butt of the joke behind his back. Quite frankly my behavior wasn't kind or godly. Well one day soon after, I was in the parking lot at the local grocery store. I was in what I thought was a wonderful position. Three cars all had their backup lights on and all three cars were near the front of the store entrance. I was going to be happy, undoubtedly I was going to get a good parking spot that day. As I was waiting to pull into a spot, all of a sudden one car started to back out and was about to hit me. I laid on my horn and the car retreated and I was relieved I didn't get hit. The car whose spot I wanted stayed in its place, but then the third car started backing out and even though I was laying on my horn a second time, this car slammed into me. Not a light bump but a really good jolt. The bump left a good dent on my car. At that moment, in my conscience I understood that getting a good jolt is not a joke. I sincerely hated getting slammed into. God gave me grace and I didn't yell at the driver and even graciously let her go. But more importantly, I thanked God that he interrupted me and helped me to stop joking about my husband. Though I had turned my back on that sin so many years ago, it still showed up in my personality and again I repented anew. God is an interrupting God who is willing to say, "Pardon the interruption, but you are going the wrong way and doing the wrong thing."

Further Study: John 5:14, John 6:43, John 7:24, John 20:27, Romans 14:13,

1Corinthians15:34

Special Thanks to Will Swarbrick

God Is Not Into Obstacle Courses
Understanding How God Fathers Us

The Lord is the Spirit, and where the Spirit of the Lord is, there is freedom. 2Corinthians.3:17

The Pharisees…tie up heavy loads and put them on other people's shoulders, but they themselves are not willing to lift a finger to move them. Matthew 23:4 (Jesus)

Watch out for those who…put obstacles in your way, …keep away from them. Romans 16:17

Jesus sensed that leaders in the church were making it hard for congregants to find their way to serving the Lord freely. Jesus spoke against loading people down, making them step through multiple hoops, and putting them through an obstacle course to get to the place of ministering in the church. After people break their bindings, jump through hoops and cross the finish line, then and only then are they allowed to enter into doing the Lord's work. Jesus wants us to be able to serve Him easily and freely within the community of faith. God is open armed toward all of us who are truly repenting and desiring to do the works of the Lord. God does not build obstacle courses, He does not load us down with thirty pound weights and give us zigzag formations to follow in order to make it harder for us to serve Him. God wants us to have a wide berth through which we can serve Him with abandonment to His purposes. I am not saying the Lord wants us to wander aimlessly nor am I saying we don't need to be led. But instead I am saying that He does want those of us who eagerly desire to serve Him to be given jobs to do so that we can help carry the load of kingdom work and help his kingdom expand. If you are discerning that someone in spiritual leadership seems to be preventing you from serving the Lord, by loading you down or putting obstacles in your way or other people's way, then you should avoid that leader.

God does not want His disciples being kept out of doing kingdom work. God does not demand that His disciples are completely healed before they tell someone about Jesus or lead a beginning Bible study. No, what the Lord desires is for leaders to remove any obstacles that are in the way of people who want to serve the Lord. You are not that kind of leader. You are an emerging leader who isn't threatened by other strong leaders, but instead you welcome other strong leaders working beside you because you understand we are all on the same team. You understand that everyone who is a Christian is called to make disciples and is welcome to do the works of God. You as an emerging leader desire to help others to start working in order to help God's kingdom come and His will to be done. You know it takes a willingness to be led by the Spirit of God. You also understand that there is so much work to be done and there are not enough workers so there would never be a reason to stop others from working! Leaders who are secure in their leadership skills are not threatened by others working alongside of them. God is not a designer of obstacle courses, instead He is like a landowner who wants those who are willing, to come and work His land. He is one who gives disciples freedom and wide berths to serve Him in a myriad number of ways. Be aware, stay away from those who put obstacles in your way of serving Christ.

Further Study: Matthew 5:21-48, Matthew 9:9-38, Matthew 12:1-27, Matthew 13, Matthew 15:1-20, Matthew 16:5-12, Matthew 23:1-39

God Is Into Construction
Understanding How God Fathers Us

> *Pass through, pass through the gates! Prepare the way for the people. Build up,*
> *build up the highway! Remove the stones. Raise a banner for the nations.*
> *Isaiah 62:10*

God's people are called to participate in God's great purposes of calling people to repentance, of leading people to Christ, of making disciples, and of helping to enlarge the kingdom of God. If we are leaving the past behind and pressing forward into the high calling that is in Jesus Christ our Lord, then God calls us to encourage people everywhere to receive Jesus as their Savior and engage people in calling others to get on fire for Jesus.

God does not want people being kept out of the kingdom of God but helped in easily and freely. God does not want it to be hard for the church-the people of God- to participate in doing kingdom work, in enlarging the kingdom of God and edifying the saints. All are called to participate. God does not demand that we are completely healed before we tell someone about Jesus. God does not demand that we be a preacher and be leading a church before we lead someone to the Lord. No, what the Lord desires is a person of passion who is willing to stand up for Jesus and to passionately pursue loving people into the kingdom of God. Everyone who is a Christian is welcome to do the works of God. All it takes is a willing heart.

The prophet Isaiah aptly reflected the heart of the Lord when he shouted, "Build up the highway!" God is into construction! God wants his leaders to build highways so those who are young in Christ can easily begin participating in helping to build God's kingdom. Jesus welcomes us into His high purposes of constructing His church. The definition of church is the people of God. The church is the people who have trusted in Jesus for their salvation. If your heart is set on Jesus and making Jesus known in the world, then you are welcome to begin construction. Tell others about saving faith in Jesus. Then, once you have learned how to lead others to Christ, work with your spiritual leaders to learn how to make disciples at your church, your school and in your community.

Further Study: Acts 18:9-10, 1Corinthians 1:2, 1 Corinthians 16:19

God Does Not Do Party Tricks
Understanding How God Fathers Us

So is my word that goes out from my mouth; It will not return to me empty, but will accomplish what I desire and achieve the purpose for which I sent it. Isaiah 55:11

God is intentional. God does not do party tricks. As a child I lived to entertain. When I really scored was when I made people laugh. A couple of years ago, one of my friends who I don't get to see very often came for a visit. In high school my family nicknamed her Chatty Patti. She always had a lot to say, Patti always kept the conversation going. Truly I usually played second fiddle to her verbal leads. So, one day, about ten of us were packed into my Suburban when Patti and her family were visiting here in Texas. I saw a car coming and we needed to give up the attempt to move into the lane next to us and so I shouted, "Incoming!" "Incoming!" "Abort!" "Abort!" Patti's kids talked about my line for weeks. I was put on a pedestal. I had made a funny. My intention to create joy succeeded. I had scored.

The truth is that while God is pleased with the funny, God is so much greater than the funny. He gives the funny and even delights in it, but when God shows up in a powerful way you can be certain it is not because He is performing a party trick, He is not showing up for entertainment purposes. When He shows up it is always for something so much more profound. There's something much greater going on. He shows up because His heart is uniquely entrenched in His purposes in the world and He is taking the initiative to demonstrate and speak what is important to Him. So, yeah, God does not perform party tricks. Think deeply, where has God shown up in your life in a spectacular way or in a quiet way? What was He saying to you then or to your Christian community?

Further Study: Job 34:12-15, Isaiah 10:7, Ephesians 1:3-14

Special thanks to David Swarbrick, Jr. who created the saying, "God doesn't do party tricks."

God's Heart to Defend the Weak-Love Speaks Up!
Understanding How God Fathers Us

> *Defend the cause of the weak and fatherless; maintain the rights of the poor and oppressed. Psalm 82:3*

> *Religion that God our Father accepts as pure and faultless is this; to look after orphans and widows in their distress and to keep oneself from being polluted by the world. James 1:27*

In His Word, the Lord has a grouping for those who are in need and they are the aliens, the fatherless, the widows, or the ones who are in weaker situations than what is ideal. God alerts us to also defend the poor and the oppressed because He loves them and because their situation is not good. People in these situations bear extra hardships, especially the hardship of isolation and loneliness.

There's a saying that you are only as strong as your weakest link which means if you have five people on your team and four are very strong, but one is moderately strong, then your team will only be moderately strong, because that moderate person will slow you down. The core value is to only have strong team members on your team and not allow the weak ones access. Unlike the world's kingdom, in God's kingdom, God doesn't keep out weak people but instead instructs us to care for ones who are weakened and defend ones who are poor or oppressed.

There was a television show called The Weakest Link. On the show you kept banking more and more money until you broke the chain with an incorrect answer. If you were a strong player, the chain was never broken and you won the game and won the maximum amount of money possible. In God's kingdom the community wins in a different kind of way than the world's kingdom. God wants the weak cared for and the poor and oppressed protected and defended; and that is how the community wins. Love Speaks Up to defend others. Love Speaks Up. Do not prey upon the weak. If you are old and frail then you are prone to be taken advantage of. If you are without a father, then you are missing the element of protection and provision and that makes you vulnerable. God's people are called to care for and not exploit ones in weakened situations. When ones in weakened situations are cared for then God is pleased because this is evidence that you are his disciple. God also wants us to speak up in love to protect and defend the poor and oppressed. When our Christian brother or sister is being exploited or oppressed, then we should speak up and defend them. Love Speaks Up.

A cool thing happens in high school and college, teenagers start to grow up. It is in this growing up phase where the unique people begin to share their light. You can shed light, follow the heart of God by caring for ones in weakened situations and defending the poor and oppressed. Teenagers and young adults can defend others and care for those with special needs who require special care. Listen, God wants his people to be unique. It is not God's heart that those with special needs be overlooked, but looked after. Speak Up.

Further Study: Exodus 22:22, Deuteronomy10:18,16:11, 24:19-21; Job 22:9, Psalm 82:3-4, 102, 146:9; Isaiah 1:17, 10:2, 38, 40:27-31; Lamentations 5:3, Ezekiel 34, Malachi 3:5, Matthew 26:41, Mark 14:38, Luke 20:47, Acts 6:1, 20:35; Romans 14:1-2, 15:1-2; 1Corinthians 1:27, 8:9-12, 9:22; 1Thessalonians 5:14, 1Timothy 5:3-16

God's Heart to Care for the Poor-Money Matters
Understanding How God Fathers Us

Do not deny justice to your poor in their lawsuits. Exodus 23:6

Do not go over your vineyard a second time or pick up the grapes that have fallen. Leave them for the poor. Leviticus 19:10

But now as for what is inside you-be generous to the poor, and everything will be clean for you. Luke 11:41

What you do with your money matters to God. God loves a cheerful giver and the Bible teaches us to give a tithe or ten percent of our income to the Lord's work, but He also commands us to care for the poor. How can this be, how can we do all that the Lord requires? We do it methodically, practicing and becoming stronger as we become a stronger disciple. The Lord teaches us to do good especially to the household of the faith. So the Lord's value is to first direct our efforts for the poor within our Christian community. If you tithe to your church, then your church should also be helping those in your local church body that are struggling financially due to disease, loss of job, or other situations of loss. Jesus said there would always be poor among us, but He also taught that as one gives to the poor, then one's treasure in heaven increases.

When you are young, you want to get many presents. I am not against receiving presents, but we need to be aware of what our focus is. What are you focused on, giving or receiving? Rather than focusing on getting things, Jesus wants us to focus on giving. Jesus said it is more blessed to give than to receive. It is a joy to give and Jesus wants us to be careful to make sure that the needs of the poor are met. Jesus wants us to share with others who are starving. Now, let me say a word of caution here, you will be asked to give repeatedly through your entire life and you must be able to give an answer of no, I will not give to you. Why do I say that? I say that because a huge number of people will ask you for money including the firemen, United Way, girl scouts, boy scouts and on and on and on. We simply cannot give to everyone who asks us for money. Many years ago I heard a Christian teacher teach people to say, "I already have my chosen charities that I give to." This saying has worked perfectly for me through the years and I have used it as a response over and over again. I give to my local church and to others as the Lord leads, and I try to remember to be kind and helpful to the poor as opportunities arise. I also regularly say no to people I choose to not give to and not feel bad about it. We cannot give to everyone.

Additionally, we can give presents but we should also give presence. To be shaped and molded so that our presence is a gift to others is a beautiful life accomplishment. Who we are, who we are shaped into is the greatest gift we have to give to the poor and the suffering, to our spouse, to our family, and ultimately to the Lord's work in the world. To be the Lord's mouthpiece, to be a blessing, to be an encouragement, honestly it doesn't get any better than that.

Further Study: Leviticus 23:22, Leviticus 25, Numbers 13:20, Deuteronomy 14:22-15:23, Psalm 41:1, Matthew 25:36, Acts 20:35

Ambassadors, Children of the King

Understanding Who I am In Christ, Identity Matters

If God is for us who can be against us? It is God who justifies. Romans 8:31-33

We are therefore Christ's ambassadors, as though God were making his appeal through us. 2Corinthians 5:20

Dear friend, if you have believed on Jesus, if you have trusted Him with your life and taken Him as your savior, then you must know that you are now indeed in a special family. Most importantly, your name is now written in the Book of Life. You now belong to a heavenly kingdom. Listen, not just anyone can be related to a king, but you are. You are now an ambassador for Christ. Think about what it means to be a United States ambassador. Imagine you are the U.S. ambassador to Germany. Any official dealings that the U.S. has with Germany you are told about. You talk to the German officials about what the U.S. position is. When you understand the German's position you talk to the U.S. government to give them feedback. And when it is of national importance the president gets involved and asks you to come in and meet with him or the Secretary of State. You are in the kingdom of God and the Bible is the instruction manual that lets you know how the kingdom works. Now that you have decided to follow Jesus you've got a special place. Don't believe for a minute the lie that you can't be utilized. God wants to utilize you as His dignitary here on earth. The devil wants you defeated, he doesn't want you to understand that you are Christ's ambassador. In God's kingdom, no one can bring a charge against you. The past is the past and you can begin to clothe yourself in royal clothes. You can start wearing the clothes of righteousness. You are a representative of a king. Truly believing this truth motivates us to have dignity. You are able to live a more dignified life. You can do this if you understand who you are. You have been bought with a price. You are valuable to God. You are a representative of His kingdom. Live to please Him.

Further Study: John 6:27, Galatians 4:6, Ephesians 6:20, 1Thessalonians 3:13

Cherished and Loved You Are
Understanding Who I am In Christ, Identity Matters

> *"For you created my inmost being; you knit me together in my mother's womb. I praise you because I am fearfully and wonderfully made." Psalm 139:13-14a*
>
> *"As the Father has loved me, so have I loved you. Now remain in my love." John 15:9*
>
> *"The Father loves you, because you loved me and have believed I came from God. John 16.27*

When you come to the place of knowing God and belonging to Him, then your life changes. You begin to understand who you are in God. Being in God started when you were born again. Once you are born again, then you understand the great creativity that began in your mother's womb, where God created you. As you begin to understand that God the Father created you, you also begin to know that you are a created being. You are not a god. God the Father, Jesus the Son, and God the Holy Spirit, are the triune God three in one. You as a created being, have eternity set in your heart as Solomon so wisely wrote in Ecclesiastes 3:11. There is a space in your heart where you are called to worship the creator of the universe. It is right and fitting for you to praise Him for the wonderful creation you are. Praise God for the unique you He made you to be! And again I say, Praise the Lord, you are neat.

Further, God declares you are loved because you love Jesus and believe Jesus came from God. In your belief, in your trusting and knowing Jesus, love comes your way. You are now in a secure place and this security will keep you through the storms of life. Knowing God means you have a wealth of wisdom and support for your entire lifetime. You have a resource that so many others are living without. You have the mind of Christ! Anyone with the mind of Christ understands life and experiences the security of His love! But remain in that love and do not stray from it for herein lies your security, your strength.

Further Study: John 3:16-17, Galatians 2:20, 1 Thessalonians 1:4, 1 John 4:10-11

Jesus, Love & Chocolate

Understanding Who I am In Christ, Identity Matters

"What other nation is so great as to have their gods near them the way the Lord our God is near us whenever we pray to Him?" Deuteronomy 4:7

Jesus replied: "Love the Lord your God with all your heart and with all your soul and with all your mind. And the second is like it: Love your neighbor as yourself." Matthew 22:37, 39

"You have heard that it was said, love your neighbor and hate your enemy. But I tell you, love your enemies and pray for those who persecute you, if you love those who love you, what reward will you get?" Matthew 5:43-45a

Each of you should give what you have decided in your heart to give, not reluctantly or under compulsion, for God loves a cheerful giver. 2Corinthians 9:7

Your identity is unique. You are neat. Jesus finds joy in cultivating greatness within people who are in relationship with Him. Jesus brings people to have inner beauty and freedom. Jesus helps His followers to develop a unique style that is their own. Jesus encourages artistry. Jesus encourages mathematical genius, creative writing, works in the heat of the day and songs in the night sung to children. Jesus inspires beautiful landscaped gardens, paintings and sculptures, and creative musical expressions. Jesus motivates people to work hard to pay the bills and to stoop down to care for kids in the home and neighborhood. Jesus enables hearts to be fully alive and engaged in community life. Jesus encourages people to speak up for justice, rooted in Jesus' values in communities. Because all of this wells up into a beautiful life for me, then it is my joy to glorify Jesus through the life I live. I make it my aim to keep the Name of Jesus alive in my community. There is power in the Name of Jesus. We have the presence of our Lord Jesus, no one else has a god so near them like we do.

It has been said that love makes the world go around. And it's true, it does. Our Lord taught us that love should be the central goal of our lives. Our Lord taught us that the chief aim of man is to love God and the second aim is to love your neighbor as yourself. In order to love our neighbors, we must first love God and then that relationship will overflow into loving relationships with our family and community. Love must be cultivated by investing in one's friendship with God. You can't love someone you don't know. When you know someone then you begin to understand what brings him delight and you begin to understand what pleases him.

It is in this way then that a relationship with God works itself out. It is not working to gain God's favor. No, rather it is instead blessing God, giving praise to God, desiring God, being in His presence, giving thank offerings to Him for all that He has done for us. Love for God moves from working to win Him, to instead being won over by Him and thus bearing fruit because He's won our hearts. But Jesus also taught that love for our enemies is also a goal. Jesus taught that love for enemies is a love that brings an eternal reward. Now this love for enemies is a love that is a mark of deep discipleship. Our love must be a love that extends to people who are opposed to God. Just as God loved us so we wouldn't be left out of the best friendship, so too we must become like Jesus, desiring for all to know Him and to be enriched.

Chocolate is a wonderful treat that should be a part of every diet. I love chocolate and what I love best is coconut covered in chocolate. Dark chocolate contains antioxidants. Antioxidants keep a body healthy by helping prevent cell damage. Chocolate should be given to celebrate and should be eaten at celebrations! Celebrations can occur often, we need to celebrate more. The Lord enjoys it when we enjoy the fruit of our labor and when we share the fruit of our labor with our neighbors. Chocolate has become a part of who I am. It is something I eat in limited quantities and something I share regularly with others. Sharing, giving chocolate cheerfully to others as my means allow, is how I thank Jesus for all He's done for me.

By the grace of God I now have a unique style. This is the beauty of truly, really knowing God; you can find your heart and your heart can be healed and you can become sweet hearted or gallant hearted. Speaking about Jesus, bringing a loving presence, and sharing chocolate, all of these three things are part of how I express myself in the community I live in. Becoming the best you can be, confidently liking who you are is a beautiful place to be. And you too can arrive at this destination of finding a unique style that suits you. I hope this resonates with your heart, making Jesus' Name known; loving God and man; and sharing your resources.

Further Study: Matthew 22:37-39, John 15:9, John 16:27; 1Corinthians 1:18-2:5; 1Corinthians 13, 2Corinthians 9:6-15, 1John 3:11-24

Fathered by Love-Author: David Swarbrick, Jr.

God Is Your Dad-Identity Matters
We love because He first loved us 1 John 4:19

He is love (1 John 4:8). God the Father. He embraces you. He longs to connect with each one of us; one at a time. He is purposeful about this. He sees you when you get up. He sees you when you go to bed. He understands what you think about and how you act. Before you say something, He knows what's on the tip of your tongue. He sees when you change your mind. He knows how many hairs are on your head. He thinks about you all day, every day. His thoughts about you are full and rich and precious. It's difficult to describe. Who knew someone could gain so much joy hearing your voice, considering your thoughts, seeing your face? He does. No matter where you go, He follows. When you hide yourself from people, He is there. Before you were born, you were a secret that only He knew. In His eyes, you are so much more than the sum of your parts (inspired by Psalm 139).

He wants you to have freedom (Gal 5:1). He wants you to have joy. He experienced suffering to ensure that you could have everlasting pleasures (Ps 16:11). He satisfies you. He is compassionate. He takes joy in giving you what you need and what you want (Ps 145:15-16). He doesn't want to cause you pain (2Cor 2:1). He wants you to experience intimacy with other people (Gen 2:18-22), to be confidently and securely a member of a family (Ps 68:6).

He not only wants you to be loved, but to love. To grow up, to mature (1Cor 13:4,5,11), to have the satisfaction that can only come from genuinely caring about someone (Phil 2:19-21) and putting their needs before your own (Phil 2:3-4), learning to honor others as the treasures they are (Ephesians 2:10), being happy as a clam, knowing that you and Dad, together, did something genuinely awesome. He knows your weaknesses and limitations, and has compassion on you (Ps 103:13-14). It's good to remember that we love from the overflow of having been first loved by Him.

Moses talked to God "face to face, as one would speak to a friend". The Bible is clear that we have a better covenant than Moses did (2Corinthians 3:7-12), because our relationship with the Father has been made complete by Jesus' death on the cross (Matthew 27:51). Because of this, we can all talk to Him, hear His voice, interact with Him and find rest in His presence.

God really is the Father that many of us have only dreamed about and thought we'd never really find.

I trust God more than I trust myself. If you want to be surrounded by and surrendered to a powerful father that knows and loves you intimately, look no further than knowing God the Father through the Holy Spirit. We have access to Him in His Son Jesus (Ephesians 2:18). Further Reading: Genesis 32:26, Ps 34:8, Exodus 33:11, Hosea 6:1-3, Acts 8:14-17

Sacred Promises-Author: David Swarbrick, Jr.
God Is Your Dad-Identity Matters

> *But as God is faithful, our word to you is not yes and no. For the Son of God, Christ Jesus…was not yes and no, but is yes in Him. For as many as are the promises of God, in Him they are yes. 2Corinthians 1:18-20*

God is not a Father that does nothing, or that is haphazardly strung along by our whims. He does respond to us. Before any of us were born, He anticipated us and put the Bible into writing so that we would know exactly what His intentions for us are. He has so many plans and dreams. He has intentionally gone about making promises.

I'd guess that all of us have broken our word at one time or another, but God hasn't. He keeps His word and keeps His promises 100% of the time. Understanding this creates an undeniable amount of expectation, excitement, and empowerment as we realize the possibilities that our futures hold.

In our modern society we understand the idea of "prerequisites". A known organization says, "If you do _____" or "If you have _____ money", "then you can have _____". We go to school. We get our degree. We give them our money. We know what the deal is. If we do our part, then things work out. Understanding this is empowering. It's exciting.

In the Bible there are dozens of "if-then" statements. Similarly, this gives us a reliable way of creating positive outcomes in our lives. This isn't to say we won't have hardships at times, but God is reliably moving our lives forward as we cooperate with Him, regardless of our circumstances.

Sometimes a person might make us an offer and we wonder if what that person is saying is verifiable. I've been swindled before, and I know that I'm not the only one. God is not a shady businessman. His "yes" is "yes" and His "no" is "no".

The Corinthian church's distrust in Paul's promise to visit them is apparent in these verses in 2Corinthians. Because of their insecurity, Paul has to assure them that, just as God is faithful, so Paul will be faithful as well. He also takes this teachable moment to help people understand that the promises written in the *Bible* are trustworthy. God meant what He said.

God's promises aren't of the variety of promise in which the person says "yes" but really doesn't intend to follow through, hoping the person "gets the hint". A person may do this because they want to help, but they don't have the ability to do so. God is far too powerful to ever need to do anything like this. It's always within God's power to follow through on what He has promised.

Or maybe people say "yes" but don't follow through because they are just trying to be nice or not wanting to offend or wanting to avoid confrontation. Or maybe they do it because they are "creating hope" as modern atheists have stated that fairy tales and "religion" do. Fairy tales that are not actually true don't create hope in the end. They create bitterness because they create a false hope that fails to deliver what is promised (Does anyone like being led on?). One tv character recently asked, "Are there any happy endings?" She was starting to believe that there aren't, and that everything she had ever believed might actually be a lie. How sad! And how false. God is working everything together for a happy ending for those who love Him and are called according to His purposes (Romans 8:28).

Every promise that God has made in the Bible is something that God will say "yes" to if you ask Him, or sometimes if you meet the prerequisite. That's what these verses in 2Corinthians say. They are all "yes". It's always within God's power to follow through on His word, and He always does. The promises that God has made do not simply pertain to "going to Heaven" after we die. They pertain to here and now. Luke 24:15-27 tells a story of two men that Jesus rebuked. They believed that Jesus was the Messiah, but they didn't believe other things that were written in the Bible. God wants us to believe that Jesus is the Messiah, and He wants us to believe more than that. He wants us to trust the promises that God has made in the Bible. These verses in 2Corinthians tell us that it is *in Christ* that we have access to these promises.

Sometimes the reason we don't believe what is written in the Bible is that there can be a process of waiting involved in ascertaining that which God has promised. Isaiah 64:4 tells us that God *takes action* on behalf of those that *wait* for Him.

Sometimes God has prerequisites for us. God wants us to be "doers of the word", and some of His promises happen "if" we do a particular action. However this verse in Isaiah shows us that one of God's prerequisites can be waiting for Him, not simply forgetting Him and going about our business. This doesn't give us control, but rather requires submission to Him and trusting Him personally. Jesus rebuked the men in Luke 24 because they plain and simply didn't take what God had said seriously: they didn't wait for God to fulfill His word.

Right now, in my life, one verse I am taking seriously is Exodus 33:14. God tells Moses, "My presence will go with you, and I will give you rest." This particular promise doesn't require anything from us. Many of us, including myself, have tried to find ways to "catch up on sleep" or feel restored and complete. This rest that we seek isn't found in our bed or a couch, in Netflix, or in completing checklists. It's found in the presence of God. Every day recently, I've spent time saying, "Thank you God that my rest is found in your presence. Thank you that you took the initiative to make this rest available to me and to inform me of that availability. Thank you that my access to this rest is assured because I am in Christ, because He died for me on the cross. I believe you that this promise is guaranteed, and, of course, is not a ruse. Let me experience this rest. In the name of your Son, Jesus, Amen." As I've done this, I've started experiencing a clear sense of rest from the Holy Spirit. I feel more rested when I wake up. I feel more rested when I work. I feel more rested when I am talking with people. I feel more rested when I am having fun.

There is no end to what we will see God do as we recognize the sacred promises that God has made to us. 2Peter 1:3-4 tells us that God has given us "everything we need" for "life and godliness". (You don't have to pick between enjoying life and being godly, btw). It also tells us that it is through the "precious and magnificent promises" of scripture that we become more and more like Jesus. Many times I've witnessed God heal people, including myself, as I took Psalm 103:3 seriously. Sometimes there is waiting involved. Sometimes we wait years or even a lifetime. But if we aren't waiting for God or we are ignorant to what He has for us, we're not going to see Him do much. And we will see Him do much more than nothing if we do put our hope in the reliability of His Word. What a Father we have!!

Further Study: Numbers 23:19; Psalm 23:1; John 14:12-13; Titus 1:1-2; Hebrews 6:17-19

Life That is Truly Life-Author:David Swarbrick, Jr.

God Is Your Dad-Identity Matters
You reveal the path of life to me; in your presence is abundant joy; in Your right hand are eternal pleasures. Psalm 16:11 (HCSB)

Everyone is looking for moments in life that are genuinely epic and worth getting excited about. Ideally every moment is full and rich. It's unclear who first said, "Life is not measured by the number of breaths we take, but by the moments that take our breath away."

In 1 Timothy 6:19 Paul refers to the "life that is truly life". In this verse in Psalm 16, David points out that God shows David the roadmap to this "life" that is truly life. This is great news! God knows how to experience a life that is fulfilled and He is willing to prepare us for it and to teach us how to get there.

The first thing that David says about life is that in God's *presence* is fullness of joy. He goes on to also say that in God's hand are eternal pleasures. God gives us good physical things to enjoy also: things that give us pleasure. However, it is the joy of the presence of God Himself, first and foremost, that brings us life that genuinely takes our breath away.

In the Bible there is precedent for the idea of throwing a party. In Matthew 22:1-10, Jesus compares the Kingdom of God to a wedding banquet. The father is not satisfied until the wedding hall is *full* of guests. In Luke 15, when the prodigal son returns home, God throws a party (v 22-25)!! 2Samuel 6 tells the story of an extravagant celebration in honor of the Ark of the Covenant, which represents God's presence, coming home to Jerusalem. Whether we are celebrating something physical and earthly, like marriage or children, or we are celebrating God Himself, there is a party involved.

Ephesians 5:18-21 presents a compelling picture of what a party in God's Kingdom might look like. Firstly, it says to not get drunk. It's so crucial that we understand that when we, in the Kingdom of God, are talking about a party, it's going to look quite a bit different than the world's party. It not only says not to get drunk, but it says to be filled with the Holy Spirit. Interestingly the first people to be filled with the Holy Spirit in the New Testament were thought to be drunk (Acts 2:15) because of the joy that they experienced through the Holy Spirit.

Verse 19 in Ephesians 5 also instructs us to sing to one another. When was the last time you sang to another human? There's something about being full of the Holy Spirit; being fully engaged by God, in word and in deed; that brings us out of our shell and makes us fully alive.

There's really no pressure on anyone. Actually, verse 21 tells us to submit to one another. The practice of discarding people when they are different in the way they express themselves during the party or when they have problems, rather than helping them figure out how they can join the party, is not a loving practice. We want to make space for people. Still, there is still this command in verse 19 for us to sing to one another and to "rejoice in the Lord always" (Phil 4:4).

You can see in karaoke or at a concert where people are looking to be swept away into an epic moment. There are lots of moments you very much want to avoid being swept into, but God wants us to find a way to have a safe party in His Kingdom in which people are singing to one another, as this verse commands.

Thirdly, verses 19 and 20 teach us to make music from our hearts to God and to give thanks to Him. This is the more spontaneous part of the party where we are just freely doing our own thing with God, even if others might be watching. A great example of this is found in 2Samuel 6. It tells the story of King David bringing the Ark of the Covenant to reside in Jerusalem. Theologians suggest that verse 13 means that David sacrificed an ox and a calf every six steps from Obed-Edom to Jerusalem. That distance was over 10 km. Every six steps for over 10 km David made a sacrifice. Talk about extravagance. Talk about consistency. Imagine the build up and the anticipation. All of this expectation was for the Ark of the Covenant. It was coming to rest in the city of David (v12). This scene culminates with David taking off his coat, completely letting himself go and dancing with all of his strength before God. Make no mistake, David was not being cool. He was not showing any restraint at all. He was doing the exact opposite of showing restraint. He was dancing like nobody was watching. He was letting all of his innermost hunger come out and say, "As the deer pants for the water, so my soul pants for you my God" (Psalm 42:1). He was loving God with his entire heart. We all long to let ourselves go, and dance and shout without holding back. God is the only one that is worthy of such intense devotion. God's presence is where the greatest joy and pleasures are. God's presence is where we find safety as well (Psalm 27:5).

There is more to life than a great party. Living a life of mature love in which we are simply loved, but we also give of ourselves to others, is the only way we will be fully satisfied. This is the conclusion of Solomon as well (Ecclesiastes 12:13). However, no matter how much you give of yourself to others, even when it hurts, life will seem empty without the joy that we find in God's presence. *Many* Christians have burned out living lives of serving others without being filled by the joy that comes from knowing God, living with community and enjoying life. God knows the path to life that is truly life, He wants to show it to you, and it always starts with knowing Him (John 17:3).

Further Study: Revelation 4:8; 5:8-14; Psalm 149:1-5; Psalm 98:4-9; Psalm 65:4; Psalm 90:14

You Belong-Guest Author: David Swarbrick, Jr.

God Is Your Dad-Identity Matters
Have we not all one Father? Has not one God created us? Why then are we faithless to one another, profaning the covenant of our fathers? Malachi 2:10 (ESV)

We are the people of God. Long ago, God made a covenant with Abraham, God told Abraham that "all families" would be blessed through him (Genesis 12:3). One might believe that the fact that God began with one man tells us that God is "selective". However, right from the beginning; we see that God's intention has been to include you, me, and people from all families.

The verse in Malachi draws attention to the fact that God's people had come into dissonance with God's purpose to bless all people. It happens often, today. We try to become good enough, or to show that we're good enough by excluding those that make us feel insecure. Does it really change "me" if the people around "me" change? No.

This verse in Malachi shows us that when we are faithless to one another we are profaning the covenant that God made with Abraham and the covenant that God made with His people through Jesus. God has included people in the Church by the blood of Jesus. God isn't only *our* Father. He's the Father of all that have chosen to respond to His love, which He made known through His Son, Jesus. We shouldn't treat these people as outsiders.

While it's true that one man may not be responsible for another, no man has been given the authority to turn his back on God's people. No man has been given the authority to exclude people from the family of God, not even homeless people. Not anyone. No man has been given the authority to be selective about which people to invite to God's party. We all have one Father. You do have the authority to choose who you invite into your own home (1Corinthians 11:20-22).

In John 13:3-5, we see that, because Jesus was secure in the Father, He wasn't afraid to be seen doing the work that slaves did. He wasn't afraid to be seen with poor people. He wasn't afraid to be seen with people that, because of a seeming lack of desirability, trigger people's insecurity. Unfortunately, when people act to exclude others, they are demonstrating their insecurity. They show that they understand their identity, not from the fact that God is their Father, but from who the people around them are.

Jesus gave a command in Luke 14:12-14. He said that when you throw a party, don't invite your friends…don't invite your family. Don't invite rich people. Invite the poor, the crippled, the lame and the blind.

It is the purpose of God that Jesus' disciples go out and *include people* in the family of God, and give to people that need to be given to. People who are *only* trying to hang out with the rich, with their friends, and with their family, aren't living in alignment with this purpose, and are, sadly, displaying their insecurity for all to see.

If you've been excluded by people from hanging out with God's people, God is opposed to the faithlessness that you've experienced. It isn't a reflection of who you are. It's a reflection of the insecurity that is currently present in God's people.

But you don't follow this example. Don't seek to create an exclusive crew. Seek to create a faithful crew. Go out and spend time with those that don't have much to offer you (so it might seem). Go out and include others, just as you have been included in the family of God (Ephesians 1:13).

If you worship Jesus, not only are you invited, *you belong*, and truly, the party follows you wherever you go. If you don't worship Jesus yet, *you are welcome* to check the party out; and *you are welcome to join* God's family anytime you want.

Further Study: Matthew 23:9, Matthew 25:40, Galatians 3:26-29, James 2:1-4

Jesus Died For You-Author:David Swarbrick, Jr.

God Is Your Dad-Identity Matters

> *Unjustly condemned, he was led away. No one cared that he died without descendent, that his life was cut short in midstream. But he was struck down for the rebellion of my people. Isaiah 53:8 (NLT)*

The reason that Jesus died for you is not that He had nothing better to do. He wasn't sitting up in Heaven listening to crickets when suddenly He had a thought on a whim: "Maybe I'll win a battle today for those...*humans*." Often times when we have discussed Jesus' death, we have focused on the pain He experienced, physically, emotionally and spiritually. The most important things about Jesus' death are that He rose again afterward and that His sinlessness made His death uniquely qualified to atone for the sin of the world.

It's significant, however, to consider what Jesus gave up personally. Again, it's not like He had nothing better to do. Jesus could have just sent the world to hell and created a new Adam and Eve and a new Church from scratch. Or maybe He could have just put Adam and Eve to sleep forever so they didn't have to go to hell, and then start over. He didn't take the easy way out. He didn't give up on us.

It was never part of God's plan for Jesus' life for Him to get married to a human. However, in an alternate universe in which Jesus were to get married, He would, obviously have married only one woman because He is, obviously, a righteous man. I say this to highlight what it means to be a good man. In reality, Jesus' only bride will ever be The Church.

In this alternate universe we would see that Jesus died in the prime of his life. Modern day matchmakers suggest that a man is most eligible during his early thirties, precisely the moment at which Jesus *did not* get married, but, rather, died. While it was never a part of God's plan for Jesus to get married, it doesn't mean that Jesus didn't have a longing to get married. If you want to know what type of parent God is, He's the type that sacrifices His dreams and His longings for the longings of others. It's even clear in scripture that Jesus had a sex drive (Hebrews 2:17) but He put other people's needs before His own.

Jesus died in the prime of his life. There's never been a bachelor that was as eligible as He was. Women are attracted to powerful men. This is not to say that power is the most important thing to all women. Women that follow Jesus recognize that Christ-like character, which is expressed through addressing the needs of others, not only the needs of oneself (Phil 2:4-8), is not a sign of weakness but a sign of love and something to be admired. Jesus is a powerful man that used His power to serve others at His own expense. He's the full picture.

Jesus is the first-born son (Romans 8:29) of the most powerful person in the universe: God. Based on this fact alone, Jesus would have, literally, billions of women lining up to be his wife. He is gentle and humble in heart (Matthew 11:29), He is good with kids (Matthew 19:14-15), He is great to have a conversation with (John 6:63), He likes to travel (Matthew 9:35), He likes to go to parties (John 2:1-11), He prioritizes spending time with family (John 2:12), He isn't afraid to take a stand (John 2:13-25), He does the dirty work (like washing dishes and cleaning toilets) (John 13:4-5), He likes to take walks on the beach (John 21:4), He keeps all your tears in a bottle (Psalm 56:8), He carves your name on His hand (Isaiah 49:16), He has 100% reliable healthcare (Matthew 12:15), and, oh yeah, He dies for you! (He then comes back after!!). He wouldn't have a hard time finding one thousand men to be in his wedding party. He's an unparalleled storyteller. The list goes on.

Jesus is God the Father's most successful son. God the Father chose to let His most highly favored Son die, instead of the ones that aren't doing anything or much of anything with their lives yet. In this we see that God genuinely loves His sons, and doesn't see them as a means to an end.

It's clear that, for whatever reason (Ephesians 2:10, Luke 3:38), we are incredibly precious to God, and He wanted to sacrifice Himself for us. I firmly believe that He can't recall this fact without tears coming to His eyes.

He put our future, our joy, our experience of every-day life before His own. He sacrificed Himself to save terrible people, knowing the endless possibilities that were waiting for Him at home. Happiness was within his grasp and He surrendered it for us, for our benefit.

"This is how we know what love is: Jesus Christ laid down his life for us. And we ought to lay down our lives for our brothers and sisters." 1 John 3:16

Further Reading: Mark 10:45, Luke 22:25-27, John 3:16-17, Romans 5:8, Ephesians 2:4-5

Angels and Celestial Beings

Unseen Forces

The angel of the Lord encamps around those who fear him, and he delivers them. Psalm 34:7

But after he had considered this, an angel of the Lord appeared to him in a dream and said, "Joseph son of David, do not be afraid to take Mary home as your wife, because what is conceived in her is from the Holy Spirit." Matthew 1:20

Suddenly a great company of the heavenly host appeared with the angel, praising God and saying, "Glory to God in the highest and on earth peace to men on whom his favor rests." Luke 2:13-14

We know from Scripture that angels exist. Scripture tells us that indeed angels have performed various functions since the beginning of time. Angels are active beings who do purposeful things. Angels at various times and in various places make themselves known on earth.

There is a difference between the angel of the Lord and various other angels. The expression the angel of the Lord represents direct interactions with the Lord in the Old Testament. (Smith) Two examples of the angel of the Lord include when the Lord spoke to Moses in the burning bush, and when the Lord spoke to Abraham near the great trees of Mamre recorded in Genesis 18. Abraham was moved to act quickly to share a meal with the Lord who brought him news that his barren wife would give birth the following year.

In contrast, there are many accounts of angels in Scripture including in the Old Testament where separate and unique angels serve the Lord and carry out tasks according to the Lord's directives. One example is when two angels were sent to rescue Lot's family when Sodom was about to be destroyed. There are other accounts of people being startled and stunned at the presence of angels, including Mary the mother of Jesus, when she found out from the angel Gabriel that she was to bear the Messiah. Zechariah, the father of John the Baptist likewise was startled and fearful when the angel Gabriel visited him to tell him his wife Elizabeth would now finally become pregnant and bear a son. As well, many others have interacted with angels on earth.

Entire books have been written about angels and many have given testimony of personal interactions with angels. We know from Revelations that there are angels for God's churches and that angels will play a prominent role in the end times, carrying out the Lord's commands. Angels are part of God's workforce behind the scenes doing the Lord's bidding.

Further Study: Genesis 16:7-11, 19:1,15, 22:1-19, 24, 28:12, 32:1; Exodus 3:2, Numbers 22, Judges 6,13, 1 Kings 19, 2 Kings 1, Daniel 3:28, 6:22; Zechariah 1-6, Matthew 2, Luke 1, 22:43; Acts 5:19, Revelation

Fallen Angel
Unseen Forces

> *And no wonder, for Satan himself masquerades as an angel of light. 2Cor 11:14*
>
> *If I drive out demons by the Spirit of God, then the kingdom of God has come upon you. Matthew 12:28*
>
> *The thief comes to steal, kill and destroy, Jesus came that they may have life, and have it to the full. John 10:10*

God hates evil, but He was with us when we were victimized by evil and He is with us now if we are suffering as a result of evil. Satan came and brought suffering into the world. Scripture teaches that Satan comes to steal, kill, and destroy, but God comes to bring life in its fullness. Satan continues to be our adversary today, but take heart because greater is He who lives in you, then the evil one who is in the world. Satan is called by a variety of names throughout Scripture. He is called Satan, and the devil, in addition to being called the serpent in Genesis and the dragon in Revelation. The devil has his own group of fallen angels who work for him to accomplish his purposes in the world. Jesus defined the devil as the Father of lies. He describes the devil as being evil through and through and containing no truth. The devil tempts and leads people to do evil things, such as when Judas Iscariot betrayed Jesus. Jesus opposed the devil with the power of God. God's power brings healing and goodness,while Satan's power brings evil, heartache, and suffering. The devil is the one who is our enemy on the prowl to devour us and wreak havoc. He will inspire humans to imprison Christians, yet in the end God will destroy him and cast him into the lake of fire.

If Satan opposes us, then it doesn't make sense to ever be on his side. Consider this analogy. Suppose you are a player on a basketball team or a volleyball team. You are the star player and you normally make twenty points per game. Suddenly for some unknown reason you switch jerseys and go and play for five minutes on the other team. You score points for your opponent. As Christians we can sometimes become blinded by selfishness, unforgiveness, bitterness, rage, etc. and we start to give Satan a foothold, and we give the other team points so to speak. A foothold means basically a good spot for Satan to be active, it is a firm place, a place from where future operations may be carried out. So, we should always strive to not be on Satan's side but to be on God's side.

So whereas the devil has power, it is limited power, and the Christian has greater power than the evil one because Christians are filled with the Holy Spirit. Christians are given authority over the evil one, and illness.

Further Study: Matthew 10:1, 12:22-29, 16:19, 25:41; Luke 4:1-13, John 8:44, John 13:2, Acts 10:38, Ephesians 4:27-32, 1 Peter 5:8, Jude 1:6, Revelation 2:10, 20:2,10

Principalities and Powers

Unseen Forces

> *For we do not wrestle against flesh and blood, but against the rulers, against the authorities, against the powers of this dark world and against the spiritual forces of evil in the heavenly realms. Ephesians 6:12*

> *For in him all things were created: things in heaven and on earth, visible and invisible, whether thrones or powers or rulers or authorities; all things have been created through him and for him. Colossians 1:16*

If you are wondering how we find out information about the evil one, one of the most significant places is the book of Job. Job was a man of integrity and the book of Job deals with the belief that if you follow God, then everything in your life will be all smooth and you will always be protected. However Job's life shows otherwise. At the beginning of the book, Job has everything in order, he is healthy and wealthy and he has family and friends he loves. However we also see at the start that Satan came and presented himself before God along with God's angels. Satan asked permission from God to attack Job. It is as though God so believes in Job that God knows Job's faith will withstand any test. Job's faith is in God not in his health, his wealth, or his social position. Although Job knows this, still when he suffers losses, his heart still breaks. In the midst of suffering and loss Job declares though he slay me, yet will I hope in him. Nothing will move Job from the place of faith. At the end of the book, after Job struggles with God to obtain understanding of his suffering, Job declares that previously he had heard of the Lord, but now he has seen and experienced the Lord in a profoundly new way. In the end, God exalted Job above his friends. God also restored to Job wealth and family, blessing him with seven sons, and three daughters.

So the moral of the story is that Satan can cause problems in your life as he did in Job's life. Sometimes we blame God for problems and Satan is the one to blame. Do not blame God for the things that Satan does. Furthermore, Scripture teaches us how to combat the evil one by putting on the armor of God in Ephesians 6, and how to be conquerors in Romans 8.

But the knowledge part is that there is still an ongoing spiritual battle. There are angelic beings with authority on earth and authority in heaven who are on God's side. We can see those in authority on earth, but we can't see the spiritual beings in authority who work for the Lord. We also struggle to discern whether certain people are on God's side or if they are sometimes just suffering a momentary lapse and have temporarily succumbed to the schemes of the evil one. On the flip side we must also understand that there are authority places in the kingdom of evil. We wrestle against the ones in power in the dark world, the spiritual beings who have authority in the under world. We must fervently pray to overcome the obstacles the evil one throws our way, resisting the devil at every step. But we also have the knowledge of who wins in the end. In the end, the Lord wins and the devil will be thrown into the lake of fire.

Further Study: Job 1:6-22, Job 2:1-10, Matthew 12:29, Romans 8, 2Cor 2:11, Ephesians 6, James 4:7,16, Rev 20

Special Thanks to Nathan Reeder

Why Does Suffering Occur?

Understanding Suffering

> *Now the Lord God took the man and put him in the Garden of Eden to work it and care for it. ...You are free to eat from any tree in the garden, but you must not eat from the tree of the knowledge of good and evil, for when you eat of it you will surely die. Genesis 2:15-17*

If you are asking the question, "Why does suffering occur?" then you are in good company. It is a question that is asked by people in cultures all over the world. The first thing to understand is that there are two places in the Bible where there is no suffering at all. Those two places are in Genesis and in Revelation. God created heaven and earth, He created man and woman and he placed man and woman in the Garden of Eden. In the Garden of Eden there was goodness and there wasn't any suffering. However, when Adam and Eve were in the garden, the serpent came and tempted Eve and told her that she would be like God. In this moment of temptation Eve forgot God's words that death would come if she ate from the tree of good and evil, and instead Eve chose to believe the serpent's lie that she would become more like God. However, as it turned out, Adam and Eve ate the forbidden fruit, and death did come. God was true, and the serpent was untrue.

In those moments, the course of the human race changed dramatically. This change was the point at which suffering entered the human experience. God gave Adam and Eve free will. In that freely chosen decision, sin and death and pain and suffering began. This choice was not God's choice. God did not want Adam and Eve to make that choice. God had made the Garden of Eden for Adam and Eve to live in. It was a beautiful place and a place of abundance. God's heart was for the Garden of Eden, God did not desire that man and woman be cast out of the Garden, but God did cast Adam and Eve out of the Garden for one reason and one reason only- in order to guard the way to the tree of life. If Adam and Eve went to the tree of life, as they were, then they would be eternally sinful, stuck in their sin. God blocked the path to the tree of life, so that men and women could be free eternally.

Further Study: Genesis 2, 3; Job; Isaiah 9, 10; Amos 4; Revelation 21

Will Suffering End? When?
Understanding Suffering

> *He will wipe every tear from their eyes. There will be no more death or mourning or crying or pain, for the old order of things has passed away. Revelation 21:4*
>
> *He will swallow up death forever, The Sovereign Lord will wipe away tears from all faces... Isaiah 25:8*

This is one of the greatest truths and comforts found in the Bible-the truth that suffering indeed will one day end. Jesus overcame death when he bore sin and was bodily resurrected from the dead, yet still, humanity waits for the full restoration of heaven and earth, and the resurrection of our bodies. But when we ask? We do not predict when the end will come. Jesus stated in Mark 13:32, "No one knows about that day or hour, not even the angels in heaven, nor the Son, but only the Father." As we wait for that day, we must not predict when that day is, instead we should do as Jesus said to do to keep watch and to stay alert. Still we can find comfort from the truth knowing that that day most certainly will come.

Currently, we have trials and sufferings yet we carry on warning and pleading with family and friends and neighbors, and yes, even strangers, to come to Christ; so that on that day other dear ones will be with us. In the meantime we do the Lord's work of reconciling people to God, telling others the Good News that they can find freedom in Jesus, they can find hope and renewal. There is no sin that can keep one from Jesus. For the heart that truly repents and cries out to God, there is the promise of restored relationship with God. With simple belief and with true sorrowing repentance there is no one who is hopeless. How can we neglect such a great salvation, such a wonderful gift? Peace with God comes through sincere belief and faith. The Garden of Eden will one day be restored. One day, Jesus will come and establish His reign on earth. Then after 1000 years of His reign, God will make a new heaven and a new earth and all things will be restored to the way God originally intended them to be. At that time, suffering will end forever. Until that time, we persuade men.

Further Study: Mark 13, Revelation

Why Does God Allow It to Continue? God Has Sent You a Care Package
Understanding Suffering

> *The Lord is not slow in keeping his promise, as some understand slowness. Instead he is patient with you, not wanting anyone to perish, but everyone to come to repentance. 2Peter 3:9*
>
> *Cast all your anxiety on him because he cares for you. 1Peter 5:7*

One of the biggest questions young Christians have is, Why does God allow so much pain in life? Why does God allow hardships like tsunamis and earthquakes? Throughout the Old Testament God continually allowed hardship for primarily one purpose, so that others would know I AM God. God risks pain in order to help people come into relationship with Him. The problem of pain is the central question in most cultures. Paul wrote in Acts 17:26-27, And he made from one man every nation of mankind to live on all the face of the earth...that they should seek God, and perhaps feel their way toward him and find Him. Yet He is actually not far from each one of us.

Dear Ones, God has sent you a care package. God has sent you the care package of Himself. God has promised to be available for you when you undergo suffering. You can give your anxiety to the Lord. God has promised everyone who has believed in Jesus this same care package. Suffering is the crucible God has allowed in order to restore us to relationship with Him. He is far more concerned with having friendship with us, rather than assuring that we have a perfect, painless existence. God desires that things be restored to the way they were in the Garden of Eden, but before things are restored, God wants all of us to repent and to turn to Him. If there is no pain would we seek God? Our pain drives us to Him.

Many times people will not move to the place of restoration until they have visited the place of desperation. What a tragedy for people to miss out on God's care package of relationship with Him, how tragic to miss the greatest gift of life—knowing God. Because God desires for no one to miss out on that gift, He continues to allow people to experience life without God, a broken fallen world, in order that some will seek and find Him. He desires everyone to come to Him. God risks putting people into places of desperation, so that people will risk giving up worshiping their security and seek God to find true life. What would you choose, a pain free life without knowing God, or knowing God and experiencing some pain?

Further Study: Genesis 1-3, Amos 4:6-13, Matthew 5:45, Revelation 21, 22
Special thanks to David Swarbrick, Jr.

Prayer Changes Things
Understanding Suffering

> *The prayer of a righteous person is powerful and effective. James 5:16*
>
> *...You do not have because you do not ask God. James 4:2*
>
> *...they were all together in one place. Suddenly a sound like the blowing of a violent wind came from heaven and filled the whole house where they were sitting. They saw what seemed to be tongues of fire...all of them were filled with the Holy Spirit....Acts 2:2-3*

Prayer is a powerful tool however, so many of us refuse to utilize it. So many times, God's people just simply do not pray. This is a great sorrow. All of us suffer at different times in our lives. Jesus said in the Sermon on the Mount that the sun rises on both the evil and the good and God sends rain on both the righteous and unrighteous (Matthew 5:45). So while suffering is to be expected, different outcomes are possible if you spend time in prayer and ask others to pray with you. I encourage you to take the time to pray with other Christians. The account in the Book of Acts is a powerful picture of what a praying community rather than a non-praying Christian community can experience. A praying community can experience the power of God. A non-praying community will experience life without power. It is God who brings life and power to the Christian experience, but we have to want Him.

So the question must be asked, do you want God, do you really want Him? Because, dear friend, this is a great truth, God really wants you. If you want God, then you can plead for mercy and find deliverance in your day of need. In Daniel chapters two and three, Daniel was facing suffering and had been sentenced to death. Daniel went home and got three of his friends to pray to God for mercy and help to reveal the mystery of King Nebuchadnezzar's dream. God miraculously revealed King Nebuchadnezzar's dream and the interpretation of it to Daniel and then King Nebuchadnezzar lifted the death sentence from Daniel, promoted Daniel to a high position, and gave many gifts to Daniel.

In the book of Esther, Esther by faith called others to fast and pray for her and with her, and thus God saved the Jews from annihilation. The account of Peter's imprisonment is recorded in Acts 12:5-11. As a result of intercessory prayer, God responded and freed Peter from jail. In Luke 8, Jairus pleaded with Jesus to come to his house. This pleading was a prayer. The reason for Jairus's desperation was because he only had one daughter, Jairus highly valued this daughter, and his daughter was dying. Others told Jairus not to bother the Lord, but Jairus had faith that his prayer would bring about a good outcome and hence his daughter's life was restored.

So, we have the testimony from Scripture that prayer changed things for Daniel, Esther, Peter, Jairus', and many others. Prayer still is changing things, and prayer will continue to change things, but in order to change things you must pray! Start with an easier goal-fifteen minutes a day at least four or five times a week. Have a paper and pen by your side, empty your mind of things you have to do, focus on the Lord, and pray in the Spirit like Ephesians 6:18 calls us to do.

Further Study: Genesis 37-50, Exodus 1-15, Daniel, 2 Kings 20:6, Luke 8:40-56, Romans 8:26

Blessing-God's Purposes In Suffering
Understanding Suffering

You intended to harm me, but God intended it for good. Genesis 50:20

And we know in all things God works for the good of those who love him, who have been called according to his purpose. Romans 8:28

Dear Ones, sometimes we fear the wrong things. We need to be more afraid of God than fearing that men in power might kill our body. Jesus plainly said to not be afraid of those who can kill our body but can do nothing more than that. Which is a greater loss, to lose your bodily life or to permanently lose your eternal life? We should spend time listening to the One who has the power to throw us into hell. But there is also a great comfort from Jesus. Jesus said, "So don't be afraid, because you are worth more than many sparrows" (Matt 10:31). None of the sparrows are forgotten by God. Dear Ones, do not believe the lie that God does not care for you. Do not believe the lie that God does not have good things in store for you.

Consider the historic account of Joseph penned in Genesis, who after going through much testing of his faith was used mightily by God to deliver many people from starvation. To do great works of God, one must learn first to faithfully follow in a multiplicity of single steps of faithfulness. Because Joseph was faithful in a few things, God entrusted to him large things. Joseph's brothers sold him into slavery, yet in spite of this great evil, Joseph found purpose from God in this suffering. Joseph utilized his time of suffering to obtain training and to consecrate his heart, and thus became a great man of God. Through Joseph the noble-hearted, many, many people were blessed.

God indeed had good things, but Joseph had to believe in the goodness of God. Joseph had to learn to distinguish the difference between his brothers' evil actions, and God's benevolent intentions. Could Joseph believe that God was good, could Joseph believe that God wanted to bless him in spite of his brothers' evil? Joseph did believe God and hence there was a blessing. Know this God, the Christian God as I know Him, I testify to you He is one who desires to bless. God is good, God intends good for you, God has worked goodness for me and He works goodness for those who love Him. God desires to bless you if you are his adopted child. God is always with you. God is for you. Those who learn to distinguish evil from good in their suffering, those who allow their hearts to be trained in their suffering, and those who trust God with their suffering, will know God and see God.

Furthermore, those who suffer have this promise, "My grace is sufficient for you". God promises grace to aide the Christian who encounters suffering as a result of living in a world that rejects Jesus. Additionally, the author of Hebrews exhorts us to endure hardship because it yields righteousness and peace. This is indeed a mystery that suffering produces character development in our souls that naturally want to escape the process of sanctification. To be holy is to be God-like. To be God-like, is to be blessed. To be a person of character who is strong and secure and able to help others is a wonderful accomplishment of a well-lived life.

Further Study: Genesis 37-50, Isaiah 57:1-2, Matthew 12, 2Corinthians 11:16-12:10, 1Thessalonians 4:3-4, Hebrews 12:11

Oh God, Why Are Others Suffering? Hey Man You're Blind, But Dude I Have 20/20 Vision
Understanding Suffering

> *Neither this man nor his parents sinned, but this happened so that the work of God might be displayed in his life. John 9:3 (Jesus)*
>
> *If you were blind, you would not be guilty of sin; but now that you claim you can see, your guilt remains. John 9:41*

So some friends of Jesus had an honest thought, is the reason this child is blind due to his personal sin or the sin of previous generations? Why is this guy handicapped? So the leaders in the church (synagogue) had a different thought. The blind man was healed on a Sunday so the healer can't be of God. We need to investigate the one who heals, we need to stop this man from doing the works of God because he's doing it on a Sunday-now this has got to stop! This blind man should not be seeing. How foolish. How sad.

It's hard to understand anyone not being excited about someone who was blind being able to see. It's really hard, isn't it? Dear friends, Jesus is saying His concern is that the works of God are displayed in lives. Jesus' concern is that people know what God is like. Who is God in His innermost character? On the inside, God is a healer and He wants people to know that. God is miraculous. God is powerful. That's who He is. That's what He wants us to see. That's why He allowed a man to be born blind so that we could see what God is capable of. If you have a physical imperfection or illness, don't let it go to waste. Use it for God's glory! Ask God to glorify Himself and heal you so that others may see and know God in all his majesty. Engage others in praying for your healing. I heard a sermon on this once and the question was posed, "If you get 10% better is that better?" Yes of course it's better. But there's a lot of skepticism about healing in the church. There's a discomfort there about being associated with "those types of Christians" who believe healing is possible. There's also discomfort there because people who believe in healing don't always get 100% healed. But the Psalmist said, God heals our diseases. Sometimes we just don't realize that we need to not just give the doctor credit or God working through the doctor, but plain and simply we just need to give God credit for healing in our lives. Thank Him for whatever amount of healing you get. Praise Him.

Further Study: Job 1:10-2:6, John 9:3, John 11:4

Special thanks to Ron Parrish and David Swarbrick, Jr.

What Am I To Do With My Own Suffering? Tears In a Bottle
Understanding Suffering

> *You have kept count of my tossings, put my tears in your bottle. Are they not in your book? Psalm 56:8 (ESV)*

What a comfort to know that God is aware of the hardships we have experienced in our life! Not only does God know, He keeps our tears and a record of our misery stored almost as if they are a treasure. God wants us to bring our hurts to him. God loves it when by faith, we cry out to Him. God is pleased by faith. Isaiah 40:31 states, Those who hope in the Lord will renew their strength. They will soar on wings like eagles; they will run and not grow weary, they will walk and not be faint. As always our faith must be active. We must commit our way to the Lord and apply His word to our life. As we apply His word and walk by faith believing His word, then God will reward us. If we put our hope in the Lord for our sufferings, walking by faith expecting that God will do great things for us, then we will be renewed in strength to face the challenges of life. If we put our hope in drugs, or popularity or a girlfriend or a boyfriend, then we are not putting our hope in the Lord and we won't be able to soar like eagles. But indeed, we can soar and God desires for us to soar, but we must walk by faith telling God that we believe in Him and that we are waiting for Him to come through for us and we are waiting on Him to give us understanding about our suffering.

You must commit your ways to Him. Walk in faith entrusting Him with the tears of your life and you will see the glory of the Lord. One great saint who did this was King Hezekiah. King Hezekiah became ill and was on his deathbed. He got the news of his impending death and prayed to the Lord, reminding the Lord how he, Hezekiah, had walked before the Lord with complete devotion. When the Lord was reminded of Hezekiah's lifestyle, the Lord miraculously healed Hezekiah and gave him an additional fifteen years of life. Hezekiah called on God to be faithful to him, because Hezekiah had been faithful to God. As a result, God honored Hezekiah's prayer. Now I am not saying God is promising everyone an added fifteen years if they live faithfully, but I am saying God is a Father and he considers our requests so we should commit our situation to His care and bring our concerns to Him. We have a better chance of doing well if we are listening and learning all of the lessons we need to learn from the Lord, our master teacher.

Further Study: Hebrews 2, 2Kings 20, Psalm 6, Psalm 42:3

Suffering As A Christian-A Chain Reaction

Understanding Suffering

> *Rejoice that you participate in the sufferings of Christ, so that you may be overjoyed when his glory is revealed. If you are insulted because of the name of Christ, you are blessed, for the Spirit of glory and of God rests on you.*
> *1 Peter 4:13-14*

> *Do not be afraid of what you are about to suffer. I tell you, the devil will put some of you in prison to test you, and you will suffer...Be faithful, ...and I will give you the crown of life. Revelation 2:10*

The idea that God calls us to share in His sufferings is a difficult concept to grasp especially as a young Christian. Some suffering comes because of our willingness to be identified with Christ and our willingness to die to the flesh and to live to the Spirit, so that God will be known in the world. As we become like Christ, many will be drawn to Christ through us, and others will be repulsed and hate us. The Bible is clear that Jesus, causes a chain reaction, and Jesus lives in us.

The more we are known publicly as a Christian, the more we share in the joy of helping others know Jesus, and also share in the rejection of the world, just as Jesus did. Now every Christian's public confession of Christ produces a chain reaction. This chain reaction has the potential to be used mightily for the proliferation of God's kingdom. Let us spur one another on to having a chain reaction for the kingdom of God to grow powerfully. Now, suffering is never to be sought out, and we don't desire it, yet when it comes it should be utilized. We have Jesus as our example as the one who did not retaliate when others mocked him, and He didn't make threats either. His body was broken in order to bring healing to us. Likewise, learning from our master teacher, we rejoice that we have an example to follow when suffering as a Christian comes to us, and that we, like Jesus, can help others heal.

Paul boldly said, "I have been appointed a herald, an apostle, and a teacher and that is why I am suffering." Leaders should not be surprised to find that they are called to suffer, because they go first onto the battlefield, not last. Both Peter and Paul, apostles to the Jews and Gentiles, like common criminals, suffered stints in prison and were eventually martyred. These were the early leaders of our faith! Do you desire to be a Christian leader? If so, you have desired a good thing, but then, arm yourself to endure suffering as a soldier of Christ. Be willing to allow for a chain reaction that will bless many people but will also repulse others as you stand unswervingly for Christ. Those who are called to proclaim the name of Christ in hostile lands are to be cared for. Demas, Phygelus, and Hermogenes all deserted Paul and this was not good. Furthermore John warned the early church about Diotrephes who sought to throw out of the church those who wanted to serve missionaries. The Apostle Paul entreated Philemon to prepare a guest room for him, and blessed Onesiphorus for being identified with Paul even though Paul was imprisoned. Paul blessed Phoebe, Priscilla and Aquila, and Mary for helping Paul with his missionary pursuits. Paul also blessed his relatives, Andronicus and the female Junia who also were thrown in prison and shared in Christ's humiliation.

John the beloved, blessed Gaius who looked after the brothers who were spreading the Gospel. Those who follow Jesus closely must be willing to be identified with those who suffer for the Name to be known throughout the world. May God help us to endure, to stand firm, to be found faithful throughout any time we are called to suffer for Him, and may God help us to aide any within our sphere of influence who are bringing the Gospel into hostile areas.

Further Study: Isaiah 52-53; Jonah 1-4; Romans 8:18-27, 16; 2Corinthians 11:16-33; Philippians 3:1-11; 2Timothy 1:15, 2 Tim 2:3-13, 4:10; 1 Peter 2:18-25, 4; 3 John

Special Thanks to N.T. Wright

Do I Have to Admit I Need Help?

Healing Matters

> When Jesus saw him lying there and learned that he had been in that condition for a long time, he asked him, "Do you want to get well? ...Get up! Pick up your mat and walk." John 5:6-8

> Jesus said, "It is not the healthy who need a doctor, but the sick." Matthew 9:12

> He had compassion on them and healed the sick. Matthew 14:14

Dear friends, if you are sick in your body, your mind, or your spirit, Jesus has compassion for you. It is not as though Jesus looks on you with disgust or blame. Rather Jesus desires for you to be whole. The Gospels record instance after instance of Jesus pausing, helping, touching, praying, and giving to those who are suffering from a myriad number of ailments. There is no doubt that he was the Messiah, a suffering servant who entered into the pain of others in order to enrich them with His power, mercy, comfort and healing. Make no mistake Jesus is a healer and he heals people who cry out for it. He himself is available as a balm to make the wounded whole. But interestingly Jesus asks a profound question-"Do you want to get well?" Well, wow, the question itself is deeply profound because we assume everyone wants to get well right? Or do they? Why in the world would we want to stay sick? Is being sick working for us somehow? What exactly are we getting out of it?

But if you're tired of being sick, if you're willing to admit you need healing, the Scriptures tell us to go to the elders and get prayed over. Blessed are you if you are longing for body, mind, or spirit restoration. Blessed are you indeed for He has healing in His wings. He is here for us presently to begin to heal us. Sometimes our souls are devastated from sins we've committed ourselves and sometimes our souls are devastated from the sins others have inflicted upon us. Sometimes our bodies are suffering from excesses of food, drugs or alcohol. Sometimes we have physical problems due to no fault of our own. No matter what the circumstance, He is a God who can make the wounded whole. Begin your answer to Him today, tell him, "Yes Lord, I want to get well, please heal me." Then get moving. The Lord gave three orders of actions to take. Get up. Pick up your mat. Walk. Healing often follows the action of moving in what strength has been given to you. Get up. Get moving and get prayed for. The Lord expects us to move and exercise the faith that we already possess in the strength that we have.

Further Study: Psalm 103:1-3, Gospel of Luke, James 5:14

Hope For Your Life
Healing Matters

> *And now these three remain: faith, hope, and love. But the greatest of these is love. 1Corinthians 13:13*
>
> *Though he slay me, yet I will hope in Him. Job 13:15a*
>
> *A bruised reed he will not break, and a smoldering wick he will not snuff out. In faithfulness he will bring forth justice…In his law the islands will put their hope. Isaiah 42:3-4*

Dear Ones, from all outward appearances, Job had to have been one of the most pitied of all men. He lost so much, yet Job exercised incredible faith. First of all, Job's oxen and donkeys were carried off, then fire destroyed his sheep, then his camels were stolen and finally he lost all of his sons and daughters in a windstorm. Job exercised tremendous faith, he tore his clothes and grieved and mourned, yet the Scriptures declare Job did not sin by charging God with wrongdoing. Job in the midst of tremendous suffering, fell to the ground in worship and praised the Lord.

Much can be learned from this book of faith, where Job's friendship with God moved to a new place in the midst of suffering tremendous loss. Job put his hope in the correct person. Job's hope was in God. Sadly so many, many times we put our hope in the wrong thing or the wrong person. Misplaced hope can result in disillusionment. We must be careful to place our hope in the person of God, rather than people or things. If you are suffering from disillusionment or despair, it may be because you are hoping in the wrong thing.

I want to encourage you that whatever you are facing, there is hope for your situation. Whenever I feel hopeless I try to remember Betsy and Corrie Ten Boom and their vibrant faith in spite of suffering in a concentration camp during WWII for rescuing Jews from the Nazis. After the war was over, Corrie, who had lost many family members during the war including her precious sister Betsy, went back to Germany and preached forgiveness and the Gospel of reconciliation to many Germans. Corrie preached to the Germans responsible for putting her into prison and the ones responsible for killing innocent Jews and the ones responsible for killing Christians who worked to save Jews. It is always good to consider others who have suffered in order to get our eyes off of ourselves. We can also of course consider Jesus who also suffered and provides hope for any situation. So if you are facing personal tragedies, take comfort, the Lord surrounds his people (Ps 125.2). If you are facing injustice, then work for justice, but put your hope in God's final justice when He comes to judge the living and the dead. If you are facing your struggle with sin and are discouraged at your lack of holiness, remember blessed are those who hunger and thirst for righteousness, for you will be filled (Matthew 5). Personal internal freedom comes to those who continue to put themselves in the presence of God looking for help and deliverance from Him. I encourage you today, to continue to hope in the Lord. Quiet your heart and ask the Lord if it's possible you are hoping in someone or something other than Him, if you are, then repent and move instead to hoping in the Lord.

Further Study: Job, Psalm 34:7, Luke 11, 2Corinthians 4:1-2,
Special Thanks to David Swarbrick, Jr.

Good Versus Evil-Use Your Sniffer!

Healing Matters

> *Love must be sincere. Hate what is evil; cling to what is good. Romans 12:9*
>
> *Woe to those who call evil good and good evil, who put darkness for light and light for darkness, who put bitter for sweet and sweet for bitter. Isaiah 5:20*
>
> *Now the Berean Jews were of more noble character…for they…examined the Scriptures every day to see if what Paul said was true. Acts 17:11*

Knowing the difference between good and evil is a good thing. It is a skill that takes time to learn. It is as though we must put on our truth noses to sniff out whether something or someone is working for good or for evil. We must use our sniffer. The first skill to acquire is to be able to sense evil and good accurately. The question we have to ask about someone who we are not sure about is, Does what they are doing line up with what they are saying? The Lord says we must be doers of the word and not hearers only. The Lord wants us to practice what we preach. Is this person actually practicing what he is preaching? Is he doing it? In line with that, if we feel unsure about someone, about someone's character or activity, or about some idea, we must also ask if what is being said or being done lines up with the Word of God? Is this activity a Christian activity or does it line up more with being a secret and shameful activity? Is the message or idea being presented in line with Scripture or is someone trying to use human reasoning to pull you toward some idea or activity that your conscience is alerting you to avoid? Proceed slowly and with caution before you make judgments. Judge slowly and with caution especially if something doesn't just "smell right". If something smells fishy, it usually is fishy. Oftentimes it doesn't take a nuclear physicist to figure it out, but sometimes it is tricky because Satan himself masquerades as an angel of light.

Secondly, once we can determine what is good and what is evil, we must then learn to reject all that is evil. The battle continues on, the war is still being waged on earth. We must choose to side with God. Not accepting evil is a good thing-that is how we side with God. God does not want us to participate in evil deeds, He does not want evil men to succeed and God does not want evil men to get away with evil deeds.

We don't have to look far to see that the battle still rages on and there are still victims. We know God wants good to reign and so we must be about goodness. Jesus is the victor over sin and death, but He wants us to partner with Him to bring His kingdom on earth in its fullness. To bring God's kingdom on earth means to be like Jesus, to bring Jesus' goodness with us wherever we go. Learn to hate the correct things. Learn to hate the correct things. Learn to hate evil. God is not wicked. God is good. So in summary, if it's evil it needs to be restrained. God restrains evil to protect people because people are worth protecting. If you are in a situation where evil is having free reign then God hates that and you must also hate it. I am calling you to not be on evil's side. You cannot tolerate evil in your presence because God does not tolerate evil. As you learn to love righteousness and hate evil, then God will give you joy and that joy will propel you into doing even greater works of God.

Further Study: 1Samuel 25:3, Psalm 37:27, Matthew 7, Hebrews 5:14, 3John 11

Good Versus Evil-Love the Correct People
Healing Matters

You love those who hate you and hate those who love you. 2Sam 19:6

Sometimes it is hard to accept the truth about people who you expect to love you but in reality they don't love you. King David struggled with this because there were a number of people he was close to who worked against him. To begin with King Saul was the first Jewish king. King Saul was David's king when David killed Goliath. Also, David was married to Saul's daughter. You would expect then, that King Saul would be for David, but in reality he wasn't. Throughout David's life, Saul repeatedly tried to kill David. Additionally, David's third son, Absalom, conspired against his own father King David! While David's kingship survived the rebellion by Absalom and his followers, Absalom died and King David lost his son.

The truths of the extreme sorrows of King David are difficult for the human heart to imagine. King David had to be careful not to be close to Saul or Absalom. Not everyone who is biologically related to us is for us. You must know who is a true friend, separate from biology. Yes we are called to love everyone, but we must be careful to avoid close friendships with those who are opposed to us. It is painful when these separations are within biological families.

Jesus has a radical view of family. Jesus said that his true mother and brothers are those who listen to God's word and put it into practice. Jesus valued discipleship, true friendship with God. Jesus calls us all into friendship with Him and true friendship sometimes has the cost of ending up on the other side of people who aren't as good of friends with God as they claim to be, because dear friends, who we are friends with matters. It is not as though we seek to be separate from others, it is just that we always must try to remain on God's side, no matter who is left or who is not left on that same side with us. In King David's life, he had to be careful to ally himself with those who supported God's established kingdom, because those who sought to kill David did not support his kingdom. Likewise, as Christians, we need to be careful to remain on Christ's side, despite the familial or political cost.

Further Study: Life of David-1 Sam-16-2Samuel 24, Luke 8:19-21, Galatians 6:10

Setting Boundaries on Self-God Is Not Scrooge
Healing Matters

Anyone who has been stealing must steal no longer, but must work with their own hands, that they may have something to share with those in need. Ephesians 4:28

Dear Friends, we must stop doing the things that God says are not good. He says they are not good to warn you and to keep you from getting hurt. God is not Scrooge. God loves to bless people, to give people good gifts. God is into blessing. He wants to get you into a place where you are excelling. He wants to get you to a place where you are soaring. Do you want to be like that eagle that soars? That's what God wants for you. If you don't believe God wants good for you, then you believe a lie. The devil seeks to steal, kill, and destroy. God seeks to bless. He loves you deeply dear friend. I tell you the truth. Jesus died for you so that you could live Big. God wants you to have a big life. God wants you to be profound and filled with wisdom. God wants you to excel and to embrace beautiful ideas. As you fill your mind with His greatness, you become great.

But you do yourself a disservice practicing bad habits. Are you habitually filling yourself with television shows, websites, and movies that don't edify? Are you smoking anything at all? Are you sleeping and eating excessively? Are you neglecting exercise? Or, are you being resourceful so that you have the capacity to bless others? Are you developing your talents so that you become a blessing to others? Paul exhorts us in 1Corinthians 10:23 that not everything is beneficial or constructive. In other words, sometimes we bring suffering on ourselves because of our own choices.

Listen, if you are not restraining yourself and if you are letting yourself do too much of what feels good in the short term, then you are hurting yourself and you need to set better boundaries on yourself. You need to be more disciplined. You are too valuable to waste. You have a tremendous capacity to grow to be a tree of blessing to others. Dear friend, set limits on what you allow, so that you will grow into all you can be. I plead with you, please do not add more suffering to your life than you already have. This is what Satan wants you to do. Bad choices will only add up to more suffering for you.

If you have suffered and you are mad at God about it and you smoke things, and you overeat, and you yell and scream then you bring added suffering upon yourself and you are choosing suffering in your life. Dear Ones, please stop choosing suffering if you don't want to suffer. Is your suffering self-inflicted? If so then stop doing those things that are making you suffer. Don't blame God for what you have chosen and brought on through your own choices. Dear friend, don't make your life worse. Trust the Lord, I promise you, He is trustworthy and He is able to help give you understanding for your life. He is able to give you wisdom, hope, love, forgiveness and all that is needed to have a really, truly good life. Trust Him for the hurts of your life and do not make your suffering worse with your bad choices because you are mad at Him.

Further Study: Luke 6:47-49, 1Timothy 5:13, Hebrews 10:25

Setting Boundaries For Self-Not Receiving Negative Words
Healing Matters

> *The judges must make a thorough investigation, and if the witness proves to be a liar, giving false testimony against a fellow Israelite, then do to the false witness as that witness intended to do to the other party. You must purge evil from among you. Deuteronomy 19:18-19*
>
> *Do not let any unwholesome talk come out of your mouths, but only what is helpful for building others up according to their needs, that it may benefit those who listen. Ephesians 4.29*

Some of us come from good Christian homes, we feel blessed and on some level we take our situation for granted. Others are also from Christian homes, yet they weren't the favorite child nor were they the black sheep-they were told good things about themselves and bad things, they heard a mix. Still others are not from Christian homes and they too either heard many good words said or a mix, or if possible, they even heard totally negative things spoken day after day. Whatever the situation you grew up with, there is a principle we all need to embrace and that is simply this: just because it has been said about you does not make it true. There are boundaries we have to learn to set on what assessments we allow to permeate into our soul. These boundaries are important because we are what we believe we are. The old adage, "sticks and stones may break my bones but words will never hurt me" applies here, with one alteration. Sticks and stones may break my bones and I won't allow your words to hurt me. When necessary the Christian must draw a line and reject words that are said in hate or in jealousy and not let them permeate their soul. In the same way that a scientist rejects research that conflicts with known conclusions so too, the maturing Christian must reject verbal negative word pictures which conflict with their known identity in Christ.

We are all a work in progress. Christ has set us free, we are free, and He will free us. If someone tells me I am hateful and evil then what do I do with that? I respond by saying, I am a new creation, Christ lives in me and God does not make junk. I am a child of the King and so no, I don't receive that I am hateful and evil I reject that. Now that doesn't mean a mistake wasn't made or a sin wasn't committed. But it does mean that you don't receive assessments that blatantly deny the reality of who you are in Christ. Now I am not suggesting that every time a misstatement is made about you that you should speak up, but I also am not saying you should never speak up for yourself in Christ. As much as it depends on you, be at peace with all men, but also be discerning especially with any leaders who are mischaracterizing your faithful obedience to Christ. To be wrongly labeled especially within the family of God should be taken very seriously. Learning to discern truth from error takes hard work and practice. It can and must be done and you must protect yourself from hurtful words lest they seep down into your soul, root there, and grow into a spiritual stronghold of false belief or bitterness. Because something is spoken, does not mean we should allow it into our soul. If it is evil and untrue then reject it.   Further Study: James 3, John 5:41

Setting Boundaries on Others-No, Wait, Maybe, Let Me Think About It

Healing Matters

> *There are six things the Lord hates, seven that are detestable to him;...hands that shed innocent blood. Proverbs 6:16-17*
>
> *If the woman does not consent, then you will be released from this oath. Gen 24*
>
> *Entrust yourself to Him who judges justly. 1Peter 2:23*

Dear Ones, in life youth need skills to say "yes" or "no" at appropriate times. Saying "no" requires courage especially when other people are pressuring us to say "yes". Standing up calmly and with dignity is needed in many everyday situations. Dear Ones, you must remember that it is okay to say, "No", "Wait", or "Maybe, let me think about it." We have to understand our identity and be someone before we can become someone for others. What do I mean by that? Well we know Jesus teaches us about unselfish living and if someone presses us into service for one mile, He tells us to be willing to go two miles. We simply can't lay ourselves down for others until we realize we are indeed someone. Some people will put you to the test and see if you will become their slave. Becoming a slave of a tester is not the same as loving those who God is calling us to love. And people who press upon us to join a group or follow their agenda can get us off track from doing the things the Lord wants us to do. It is the Lord we must follow. Jesus went out into the desert and was tested by the devil and He resisted the devil when the devil told him to turn stones into bread, jump off a cliff, and worship the devil. Jesus said, "No" and he was okay with saying no. Before Jesus raised Lazarus from the dead He was asked to come and He said, "Wait," and He showed up four days after Lazarus already died. When Peter told Jesus not to go into Jerusalem Jesus said, "No Peter, I am going there to die". Discipleship does not mean that you don't limit other people. There are many good things to do and we simply cannot do them all. We all must learn to say no to good things in order to be a part of the best things for us.

If someone is bothering you by repeated requests and they don't respect your answer then this is when there is a need for stricter boundaries. Some people might want to spend time with you excessively, maybe even obsessively. Saying no does not mean you are unkind, saying no

67

might be a good choice which is going to strengthen you. Being a strong leader makes you a blessing to your peers.

In addition to personal boundary setting, there is societal boundary setting, such as a police force to protect people from lawless people. Scripture tells us that God is against violence against innocents and the courts support this moral value for youth who have been mistreated. The court provides youths with protection if needed because they believe youths are valuable, and worthy of being protected.

Finally, take comfort. God knows about our imperfect family situations. God knows what situations his sons and daughters are facing. In God's family, the Scriptures teach us to not tolerate evil. Evil is different than struggling. No family is perfect and spiritual leaders can assist families to grow to be more loving over time with care and with prayer, leaving destructive ways behind. An active, alive faith must give unfair, annoying family situations to the Father, trusting and believing that He will sustain you as you continue to trust in Him for a situation which may not be ideal. Do not rebel, obey your authorities, and talk to your pastor or call Focus on The Family for free Christian counseling if you need more help. 1-855-771-HELP (4357)

Further Study: Genesis 24:1-9, Genesis 31:31, Leviticus, Judges 21, 1Samuel 2:16-17, 2Samuel 13:12, Ephesians 6, Hebrews 9:17

Healthy Friendships-Don't Burn Bridges

Healthy Relationships

Mordecai was prominent in the palace; his reputation spread throughout the provinces, and he became more and more powerful. Esther 9:4

...the pleasantness of a friend, springs from their heartfelt advice. Proverbs 27:9b

Better is open rebuke than hidden love. Wounds from a friend can be trusted. Proverbs 27:6

Do not forsake your friend or a friend of your family....Proverbs 27:10

We've all heard stories about burning bridges behind us. If we say a person burns bridges it means there is no desire to ever go back to whomever they have just left. They go forward without regard for their history and they resolve to never be in relationship again with whomever they are getting away from. When we burn bridges behind us, we fail to appreciate that our history comes to bear on our future. When a person repeatedly burns bridges it is most often for reasons they do not completely understand. To hold onto the past is not healthy, but neither is running from one's past. Sooner or later your past catches up with you and it is best to face your past, deal with any brokenness, and receive healing from the Lord. It is healthy to leave room for reconciliation of relationships, and to stay open to asking forgiveness or giving forgiveness as needed. Making peace with a troubled past takes time and care, and all of God's children are worth being cared for.

Healthy friendships mature with time and relationships in Christian community have the ability to enrich hearts and lives. Healthy friendships provide comfort in the sea of life. To learn the art of friendship making takes time and commitment. Friendships are especially important in the teen through young adult years. To make friends with others means a willingness to consider someone's input in your life in the form of receiving advice, having fun together and remaining loyal in spite of stresses that come and go in the ebb and flow of life. An example of a person who was strong enough to continually build healthy relationships was Mordecai. Mordecai had a strong friendship with Esther and together they were able to solve complicated problems that arose within their faith community. All of us need mentors and our local church should be able to assist us in finding a person who can help disciple us as needed. Holding onto relationships for extended periods of time is healthy for the soul even if friends only see each other sporadically. A sure foundation of a good friend is someone who also is a Christian and who is trying to follow Jesus. It is always good to stay connected and avoid isolation.

A good friend is one who will encourage you when you are down, but a good friend is also willing to tell you the things that are hard for you to hear. When there is a strong element of shared history, there is a strength flowing from the relationship. This strength is able to speak the truth in love, to aide you with any blind spots you might have and does not tear down, but helps build you into someone greater. Only a true friend can do this and we all need true friends.

Further Study: Esther, Ephesians 4:15, 1Thessalonians 5:11

Reconciliation-When I Mess Up
Healthy Relationships

> As you are going with your adversary to the magistrate, try hard to be reconciled on the way...Luke 12:58 (Jesus)

> Leave your gift there in front of the altar. First go and be reconciled to them; then come and offer your gift. Matthew 5:24 (Jesus)

When there is a rift we must try to mend it whether we are the antagonist or the victim. The heart of one who loves as a lover of Jesus is always, as much as it is possible with you, trying to be at peace with all men. When we know we are wrong, "I am sorry" and "I was wrong" sometimes become the hardest things for us to say, however, when we need to we must say it. A helpful technique we do in my family is we slap our head with our own hand and playfully say, "I am such a schlep! Why did I do that?" Making fun of our weaknesses helps to take the sting out of having to ask for forgiveness. If we offended/sinned against someone, then we must go and apologize. God calls us to go, to be the lead peacemaker. That is what's done by ambassadors. Ambassadors of peace humble themselves and admit when they make a mistake.

Ambassadors of peace also attempt to make things right by correcting the error. If they sinned by telling a falsehood about someone then they try to make it right by letting people know what the truth is about that person. If they sinned by stealing something from a person, then they try to make it right by giving back what belonged to that person. If they used negative words that hurt, then they will try to give words of blessing to the one they hurt with their words.

God doesn't promise that the person who is angry with you will hang out with you again. He doesn't promise that the person you hurt is going to be easy to get along with all of a sudden. What God does promise is that He will reward you if you do what He says to do. Do what He says and you will definitely find reward. Jesus told this to the crowds in the context of interpreting what is going on. The reward to the person who makes it a practice to always be reconciled to others is to have peace, deep understanding, and to have abundant wisdom.

Further Study: Luke 12:54-59, Luke 18:10-14, Hebrews 11:6

Reconciliation-When My Friend Messes Up
Healthy Relationships

> *If your brother or sister sins, go and point out their fault, just between the two of you. If they listen to you, you have won them over. Matthew 18:15 (Jesus)*
>
> *Peter asked, "Lord, how many times shall I forgive my brother or sister who sins against me? Up to seven times?" Jesus answered, "I tell you, not seven times, but seventy-seven times." Matthew 18:21-22 (Jesus)*

When there is a rift we must try to mend it even when we are the victim. In the case where your friend sinned against you, again you must go to them and try to work it out. The Scriptures exhort us to speak the truth in love, and also to forgive repeatedly. Jesus did not just say to be reconciled, He said to try very hard to be reconciled. Are you angry with someone who has hurt you? Then work at working it out. God will show you things you can do to ease the way. You can give a small gift of fruit or you can tell a joke-these little touches might help to make things less painful and show that you want to stay friendly, but the words you say can still speak that what your friend did was hurtful. You can also pray. You can make time for a visit and be humble. If they hurt you, you must be gentle knowing that you too are capable of hurting others and needing forgiveness. So once you have broken the ice, and spoken about the hurt that is in your heart, then with the Lord's help you can forgive. The most serious problem for the Christian occurs when there is sin of an extremely serious nature. (Questions about extremely serious sins should be discussed with your youth leader or your pastor.)

The important thing is that you honor God by doing what He says to do (go to your friend and try to make peace), and you look for your reward from the Lord. This is what it means to live by faith. Now I am not promising that your friend will apologize. It does not mean that your friend will change and stop hurting you. But God rewards those who live their life to Him in faith, for without faith it is impossible to please God. If you go to your erring friend then God will know that you are working for reconciliation and He will bless you for it. We must believe that God exists and that He rewards us when we do what He says to do.

Further Study: Matthew 18:15-35, Luke 12:58, 2Corinthians 5:18-19, Romans 5:10-11

God Is Into Restoration
Healthy Relationships

> ...If someone is caught in a sin,, you who live by the Spirit should restore that person gently. But watch yourselves, or you also may be tempted. Carry each other's burdens, and in this way you will fulfill the law of Christ. Galatians 6:1
>
> Don't let anyone look down on you because you are young, but set an example for the believers in speech, in conduct, in love, in faith and in purity. 1 Ti 4:12

So do you think that you have the understanding to help someone stop sinning? Well the truth is you may have the understanding or you may not, but if you do, then the Lord will give you grace to help a brother to stop sinning. Let no one despise you because of your youth. Having the correct attitude is key in being successful in helping your brother climb out of a pit he is getting himself into. Number one, remember the goal is helpfulness so that he will not feel condemned, but so that he can be restored. Now I heard a story a while back about two different men. Both of these are true stories. Both men had testimonies that they were

72

believers. Both men also had committed crimes of stealing money from their companies even though they had confessed Christ as Savior. Both of the crimes were going to come to the light and people were going to know what happened. One man committed suicide. The other man confessed his sin to his pastor, went to prison for a year and his church received him back and he repented and changed his life. Which of the outcomes reflects the heart of God? The man who confessed his sin, went to prison, repented, and was restored to fellowship in his church is the ideal way to help someone caught in a pattern of sin. God's heart is to confront sin, allow for repentance with eventual restoration to the community of faith and finally a return to ministry. It is better to deal with a sin and turn from it than to believe the lie that there is no way out. There's always a way to move forward.

Yes, it would be great if no one ever got caught in such horrible levels of sin, but it does happen. The cases in a teenager's life might not be so extreme as this example of the two men, but it also might be that extreme of a case. Someone you know could be endangering himself and it would be kind to go to him and gently warn him. Of course this must be done in love and in kindness and with prayer. Restoration is putting things back to the way they ought to be. True restoration begins with and is rooted in salvation which makes moving forward possible.

Further Study: Jeremiah 30-33; Ezekiel 33-48; Luke 19:1-10; Acts 3:21; Gal 6.1; Rev 21:1-5

Broken Families-Accept Your Losses
Healthy Relationships

> *My grace is sufficient for you, for my power is made perfect in weakness. 2Corinthians 12:9*
>
> *Anyone who loves their father or mother more than me is not worthy of me; anyone who loves their son or daughter more than me is not worthy of me. Matthew 10:37*

Sometimes we look around and we just want to be one of the beautiful people. We think, "Oh God, if only I hadn't been born into a family that was sick, if only I hadn't been abandoned as a young child, if only I wasn't an only child, if only my dad hadn't died when I was young, if only I wasn't diabetic, if only I was adopted and not in the foster care system, etc. The truth is we are in the situation we are in now. You must face the truth of your life however painful it is. When you have the courage to face the truth, then you will find grace to accept the truth of what or whom you have lost.

We can gain strength from the example of the Apostle Paul. From Scripture we know the Apostle Paul was faced with a physical problem of some sort. We are not given his diagnosis. What we do know is that God had the power to change Paul's situation, but God did not. Now that's tough. We have to sit with the knowledge that God sometimes chooses to not change our situation. What do we do with that? What we do with that is we begin to trust that God has purpose for us in allowing suffering. That purpose is to drive us to Him so that we don't miss out on knowing thee best friend we could ever hope to have. We begin to believe that God is truly good, that all things work together for good, to those that love God as Romans 8:28 states. We begin to trust God and give Him a chance. We step out in faith and we say a prayer giving Him all of our sorrows and all of our disappointments. We cry out to the Lord, give Him our losses, and we begin to trust Him one step at a time. We accept our losses and trust God. Where we find emptiness due to loss, we are then filled up with God.

The author of Proverbs enjoins us to trust in the Lord with all our heart and lean not on our own understanding. If you commit all your ways to Him, then He will make your paths straight. Listen, God is trustworthy. Does a child understand that running in traffic could kill him? Does he like it when a parent restrains him? No a child does not understand about traffic, but eventually the child learns that the parent who restrains him from running in the street was a good trustworthy parent. Similarly, God trains us to come to Him and to not "run wild in the street", but instead to mourn our losses from evil and from the fallen world, and instead to trust the Lord for our losses and accept our losses. When you crown Jesus as Lord of your life, your most treasured friend, then the Lord eases your burden, He becomes your forever family.

Further Study: Proverbs 3:5,6; Matthew 10:32-42

Broken Families-Letting Go

Healthy Relationships

> *While they were in the field, Cain attacked his brother Abel and killed him. Genesis 4:8*
>
> *"I hate divorce" says the Lord, the God of Israel, "because the man who divorces his wife covers his garment with violence," Malachi 2:16*

Many people in the family of God are suffering now with broken families. Some breaks in families are due to addictions; murder and hate; or adultery and lust. Family breaks cause confusion and chaos for spouses and children. Broken families are not God's best. We know the goal is to keep families intact but God knows it is not always possible. If you are in a broken family you have three challenges: accepting your losses, letting go of destructive connections, and bonding to the people God wants you to bond to.

Letting go of biological connections if they are destructive and evil is hard. I hear you saying things like, but she's my mother, but he's my brother. Listen, if you are in God's family then you will know God's ways are not to destroy people but to protect and care for people. You are worth protecting and you must trust the Lord to help. Your heart must be committed to Jesus first, not biological connections. You must learn to love what Jesus loves and if people you love are siding with evil, then you remain on Jesus' side, no matter who is on what side. You stay with Jesus because you, you always stay on God's side even if some of your friends or relatives are currently doing the wrong thing! Is there someone I need to let go of who has hurt me? Do pray for people, for your prayers accomplish much, but don't side with people who are doing evil things. Loosen your attachments to any who would draw you away from Christ or draw you to doing things that are against your conscience. Let go, release your attachment to destructive individuals, people who are dangerous and people who are opposed to God.

Further Study: Acts 6:9, Philippians 1:27-30, 1 Thessalonians 2:2, Hebrews 12:3

Broken Families-Bonding to the Right People

Healthy Relationships

> *"My mother and brothers are those who hear God's word and put it into practice."*
> *Luke 8:21*

Jesus defined family in a new way in Luke. He defined His family as a group who transcends biology. God is not saying to reject your family. God is saying, Listen, spiritual connection is even stronger than biology. This is your family, the family of God who are following God and putting away evil. This is your forever family. This is your family who you will be making eternal dwellings with. People who practice evil continually and never repent are not going to be in your eternal family. Yes God wants everyone to come. Yes God opens wide the door for everyone to come. Yes God is allowing life to go on hoping that everyone will repent of evil ways and follow Him. That is the heart of God. And we should keep earnestly praying for all those members in our biological family to follow Jesus. We should earnestly strive to show them the love of Christ.

But, now your focus is to be on your new family members who follow Jesus, some of them may be biological family members, some may be neighbors and some may be people you barely know. Be determined to stay close to God and close to those who are not only listening to God, but those who are listening to God and obeying God. Those who in actuality are doing the things that God says to do are people you should be close to. Bond to other Christians, and pray earnestly for those who are not Christians to come to know Jesus. Bond to the correct people so that you do not go astray. Bond to the correct people so that you begin to understand the fellowship of the saints and experience blessed alliances.

Listen, Jesus is victorious, He already has won. And if we battle in prayer and in practice for Jesus to be central in our families, in our church, and in our community, then we will have victories and we will see people come to Christ and some of those we love and care about will one day honor Jesus as Lord alongside of us.

Further Study: Acts 2:38-47, 1John 1:1-10

Healthy Families-Captain Obvious
Healthy Relationships

> *Children, obey your parents in the Lord for this is right. Ephesians 6:1*
>
> *Stand up in the presence of the aged, show respect for the elderly and revere your God. I am the Lord. Leviticus 19:2*
>
> *You know the commandments: "You shall not murder, you shall not commit adultery, you shall not steal, you shall not give false testimony, you shall not defraud, Honor your father and mother." Mark 10:19*

We all like superheroes. Superheroes help us because they remind us of many great things to which we all aspire. We like it when our culture inspires us to have courage. It is good for us to imagine rescuing others and doing noble things. Pictures fuel the imagination. Words move our hearts to dream of having courage to do seemingly impossible feats. Captain Obvious is not a superhero, but he is a tv personality. You've heard of him, haven't you? My son talks periodically about Captain Obvious. Captain Obvious states things that are so obvious, yet they still need to be said. It's kind of like those pictures you looked at when you were a little kid, where you needed to find items that were drawn inside paintings. Essentially there were pictures hidden within pictures. The hidden pictures were not obvious at first, but later when you looked at the answer and you could see things more clearly it seemed so obvious.

Obeying your parents is like that. Sometimes it's obvious after the fact that it was important to respect your parents and you should have listened to them. When your parents have done things for you, you need to give them thanks. This is something Captain Obvious would remind us to do, even though many of us know it. If we aren't careful we might take our parents for granted. Parents, whether biological or foster or adoptive, all sacrifice for their children and in a way that's heroic. If we don't give thanks for the parents who really do the work of caring for us physically, emotionally, and spiritually, then we are not doing what God has called us to do. You must speak thanks because your parents have done more for you than anyone else in your life. Yes, it's obvious they're supposed to do that work, but you still must meditate on just how many hours and hours of work they have heroically done on your behalf.

It was in vogue in the 1990's to teach appreciation to children. To accomplish this task, public schools had students carry baby dolls around with them for entire days. These dolls represented what it was actually like to have a baby and care for a baby. Students would have to get up in the middle of the night for nighttime feedings and also be responsible for caring for the doll throughout the entire day, in order to mimic what parenting was like. Although, the purpose may have been to deter teen pregnancy, it also simply taught that being a parent is a lot of work. So, if for no other reason, tell your parents thanks for caring for you because you understand it is hard work. I hate to be so obvious about this, but when you say, "Thanks Mom and Dad", you are being obedient to God and growing as a disciple.

Further Study: Exodus 20:12, Deuteronomy 5:16, 21:18-21; Ruth 2:11, 2Kings 3:2, Esther 2:7, Proverbs 4:3, 17:6, 17:25, 19:26, 23:22, 23:25, 28:24; Mal 4:6, Matthew 19:19, Luke 1:17, 2Corinthians 12:14, Ephesians 6:2-3, Colossians 3:20, 1 Timothy 5:4
Special Thanks to Eric Swarbrick

Healthy Families-Blessed In Order To Bless Others
Healthy Relationships

> *I will make you into a great nation, and I will bless you; I will make your name great, and you will be a blessing. Genesis 12:2*
>
> *Land that drinks in the rain often falling on it and that produces a crop useful to those for whom it is farmed receives the blessing of God. Hebrews 6:7*
>
> *Do not repay evil with evil or insult with insult. On the contrary, repay evil with blessing, because to this you were called so that you may inherit a blessing. 1Peter 3:9*

In the ideal Christian family, Christ is the head of the parents, and the parents are the head of the children. In Christian homes, where Christ is the head of the house, the family understands their need for Christ. There isn't any argument, God is the head and the family follows God.

Servant leadership is the key to healthy family life. Fathers take the greatest burden here to serve because of the way they're built. The male physique allows for greater physical productive work than the female physique. Because of this servant leadership, care must be given to honor the father. Sadly in our culture, men are not receiving the honor they should receive. A father's blessing to a family is important. Consider the hardships families face without a father. Now I am not saying that mothers aren't important. But it is important to recognize that most fathers work hard for their families and that they should be blessed verbally for that hard work. To act as though a father's contribution or a mother's contribution doesn't matter is to sin. Blessing your parents is important.

If you struggle with blessing your parents, your siblings, or your friends, make sure you are spending time receiving from the Lord. In order to be a blessing you must be receiving blessing from the Lord. Also, consider God's example. We serve a God of blessing. God blessed Abraham and made his name great, and made Abraham a blessing to others. God can and wants to do the same for us. God blessed us through the redemption we receive because of Jesus' work of redemption on the cross. God blessed all of us who are in Christ, by adopting us into his family. Further, God has poured out his spiritual blessings on us by giving us spiritual gifts. God is thee God who blesses and so we must become like Him, we must become people who bless others with gifts of kind words, gifts of words of thanks, physical gifts of tokens of appreciation. With each blessing we give, our capacity for continued blessing increases, and our heart finds peace and joy in fruitful relationships. We also will find our hearts moving away from unfruitful words.

A great activity to do as a family is the circle of blessing. Everyone sits together in a circle. Starting with the father, everyone goes around the circle and tells how the father has blessed them. Then it is the mother's turn. Everyone goes around the circle and tells how the mother has blessed them. Then it is the oldest child's turn and so forth until all the children in the family have had a turn to be blessed by everyone else. When we did this in our family of six, it took us about four hours to complete, but it was a life changing experience and I highly recommend it.

To be healthy, each family must learn to bless all members, each family must learn to work together as a unit, and each family must submit themselves to each others' needs as they arise. The Lord helps families rebuild places that are broken. Healthy family life takes dedication. What is essential is that you learn to bless what's good.

Further Study: Genesis 27, 49:28; Exodus 23:25, Lev 25:21, Deuteronomy 11:26-32, 28:8, Deuteronomy 29:19, Deuteronomy 33, 2Sam 16:12, Psalm 109:17, Malachi 3:10, Galatians 3:14, Ephesians 1:3

Special Thanks to David Jr.

Wholesome Living-Stand Your Ground
Dating and Sexuality

I have written both (my letters) to stimulate you to wholesome thinking. 2Peter 3:1

Those whom I love I rebuke and discipline, so be earnest and repent. Rev 3:19

Remember...you stood your ground...in the face of suffering. Hebrews 10:32

Dear Ones, living a wholesome life is the will of God for you as a teen, as a young adult, and beyond. I urge you to determine to not have sex before marriage and to stand your ground on this decision. The truth is many mistakes are made in the area of dating and sexuality. While we want to get it right, many times we get it wrong and we sin. Both genders struggle with lust, but especially males because they tend to be most interested in how girls and young women look whereas most females like to hear about how good they look. Because of this, guys are prone to focusing on picking a girlfriend based on her looks, whereas young women are prone to choosing the wrong boyfriend based on how much he sweet talks her. Knowing this then, I propose to you to be careful in your dating practices, and to learn as much as you can about people you are interested in dating in addition to how they look. Learn about the opposite gender's character, their interests and hobbies, and their pursuit of God's best for their lives as evidenced by steady growth in their relationship with Jesus and with others.

Wholesome dating for teenagers may include attending chaperoned events with parents' approval. Prolonged single dating that goes on for an extended period of time greater than six months, has an increased probability of sexual activity and should be avoided in the teen years. It is my heart that you stay innocent until your wedding day.

Listen, it is important to have fun in your teenage and young adult years. It is important for you to grow up and mature and not feel pressured to be dating a lot, and not pressured to have sex, but instead to have wholesome friendships and to practice being friends with the opposite gender. Being wholesome allows for a clear conscience, and also allows for fun, without the pressure for sex, or the responsibility of bearing a child in your teenage years. When you have made this decision, tell your youth leader or your parent. Telling someone will help you to stand your ground for wholesome living and not waver. However, if you do make a mistake, there is forgiveness. God's mercies cover sexual sin. When you make a mistake you need to repent and stay away from your wrong sexual behavior and determine in your heart not to repeat the same error. I desire good things for you, especially a good conscience so that you don't shipwreck your faith. All Christian young people should be learning about the opposite gender with their hearts and minds as they grow up toward adulthood so that they can eventually choose a mate with care.

Further Study: Proverbs 5, 6:20-35; Romans 13:13, 1Cor 6:12-20, Eph 5:3, Hebrews 10:32-39

Friendships While You Wait-Practice Asking, Accepting, and Refusing
Dating and Sexuality

> *"Listen to me. Don't go to glean in another field and don't go away from here. Stay here with my servant girls." So Ruth stayed close to the servant girls of Boaz. Ruth 2*

> *"Come out from them and be separate, touch no unclean thing and I will receive you," says the Lord. 2Corinthians 6:17*

As you grow in opposite gender relationship skills, my prayer for you is that you learn to choose well. The choosing of your lifetime soul mate is one of the most important decisions you will ever make. Along the way you must practice inviting and receiving people into having a relationship with you, and you must also practice refusing to be in relationship with people. Simple invitations should include start times and end times, mode of transportation, and should clarify any specific details concerning tickets, gear, or appropriate attire. Simple receptions should be simply a yes with a firm commitment to come or to welcome. Simple refusals should be a kind but firm no, communicating clearly whether or not the refusal is due to a lack of interest, a blocked schedule, or a decision to not be dating at all. It is kind to give information to people who have risked asking to be closer to you. Dear Ones, do not give hope for relationship where there is no hope. It is unkind to lead people on.

The best kind of dating when you are young is group dating. Please consider my advice carefully. If you can say to a person who you are interested in dating to bring along his friends to a chaperoned gathering at your school, or a youth event at your church, then more safety is provided for everyone. If you are able to welcome into your group events many instead of just one, then that is good for everyone. The old adage there is safety in numbers still holds true today. It is always a good practice to have another friend of the same gender along with you so that if a situation turns sour, you will have a friend who can call for help, a friend who can call your parents, or a friend who can help you leave a situation that makes you feel uncomfortable. Good practices for social events are to go in a group and to avoid single dating until you are dating for marriage.

Now I am not saying this as a law for you but only for a guideline. I am for your growth. I desire that you commit to a wholesome lifestyle within the framework of a Christian community. I desire that you practice inviting people, and welcoming people into a closer relationship with you and that you practice stating details of events including all pertinent information. I desire that you practice refusing to be in closer relationships with people and that you do that with clarity and kindness.

Further Study: Genesis 24, Genesis 29:1-20, Ruth

Singleness, Loneliness, Self-Stimulation

Dating and Sexuality

> *Flee from sexual immorality. All other sins a man commits are outside his body, but he who sins sexually sins against his own body. 1Corinthians 6:18*
>
> *But among you there must not be even a hint of sexual immorality, or of any kind of impurity. Ephesians 5:3*
>
> *"You have heard it was said, "You shall not commit adultery. But I tell you that anyone who looks at a woman lustfully has already committed adultery with her in his heart." Matthew 5:27-28 (Jesus)*
>
> *It is good for a man not to marry. An unmarried man is concerned about the Lord's affairs, how he can please the Lord. But a married man's interests are divided. 1Corinthians 7:26-32*

Dear Ones, some things take extra patience and study to understand. Singleness is a gift and marriage is a gift. Those who do not have the gift to remain single should not expect themselves to stay single. Some people choose to stay single in order to advance the Gospel. If you are single and desire to marry one day, then it requires patience to wait until the time is right for you to get married. The time of waiting can be a time of victory or a time of defeat. Continue to keep a contrast in your mind about what two different outcomes could look like. Waiting can be used for your personal development and as a special time to serve the Lord, or waiting can be painful and filled with sexual defeats if you can't keep your sexual appetites restrained.

The victorious choice is the one to keep in front of you. The time of being single with restrained sexuality can be a tremendous blessing in terms of your personal growth and development. This time of freedom should be enjoyed. Once you get married and start having children everything changes and it becomes more difficult to have mobility. When you're single, you can use this time to grow in your ministry skills and go on a short-term mission trip. It can be used as a time to get a bachelor's degree or a vocational degree. One could become an accomplished musician, an electrician, or chef; the possibilities are endless. However, we cannot be blind to the struggle inherent to singleness, which is of course the loneliness that goes along with being single. The Holy Spirit is a comfort during this time, yet still the sex drive and hormone management during the single years is a snare for many. It is important at this time of life to avoid fantasizing about sex and to avoid engaging in self-stimulation. The more one partakes in this activity, the harder one makes it on one's self. Instead it is better to cultivate some Christian friendships, Christian group activities, and Christian family life in order to remove the sting of singleness. Christian community life, along with spending time with the Lord, are the essential elements needed to survive the waiting period of singleness for those who intend to marry.

Further Study:1Corinthians 6, 7; Colossians 3:5, 1 Thessalonians 4:3

Principles for Choosing a Mate-Eyes Wide Shut
Dating and Sexuality

Do not be yoked together with unbelievers. What does a believer have in common with an unbeliever? 2Corinthians 6:14-18

First and foremost it is important for a Christian to marry a Christian. Please receive my instruction and do not marry someone who is not committed to Jesus. Once you are considering becoming engaged with someone you should devote yourself to prayer and ask God if you should marry this person or not. It takes discernment and prayer to figure out if a person is truly following after Christ or not. If you sense God's approval, and if other Christians close to you agree this person is following Christ, then you can choose to consider marrying this person.

Secondly you must then look at lifestyle choices. The male, due to his physicality provides the tent. What do I mean by calling the male the tent provider? If a man is a military man or a missionary, then your family will be a military or missionary family. If a man is a blue-collar worker then you will be a blue-collar family. Whatever the man's tent, will primarily be what the family is shaped by. In contrast to that, the female provides the interior and exterior community style. Women tend to define the unique interior and exterior family style. If the woman is extremely well educated and career oriented, then your family style may involve smaller numbers of offspring, or desire for a nanny situation. It could mean a quieter less dynamic family life. If the woman is extremely into child bearing and loves large family gatherings it might be her desire to have an exceedingly large family which would demand a greater amount of financial provision and less ability for her to contribute to family finances. The woman might also be an introvert who in general prefers music and books, or she might be a high level social engager with a great capacity for making a myriad number of friends.

Finally these lifestyle "tents" and "interior and exterior community styles" should come with expectations that match realities. What I mean by this is that if you choose to marry a military man, you should expect to move around from place to place. If you choose to marry an introverted woman, you should expect to have a quiet home life. Do not go into marriage with your eyes wide shut and with unrealistic expectations.

Many people think that love is enough to get married, but I say unto you that you really should marry a Christian, understand their likely tent and style, and you should like the person you are planning on marrying. What I mean by this is that you should not be so in love with the idea of being in love that you are blind to obvious things, which in later years you will regret. Once you choose, it is for life, so choose well.

Further Study: Genesis 19, Genesis 29-30, 1Samuel 25

Dating For Marriage
Dating and Sexuality

> *"What if the woman will not come back with me?" "If they refuse to give her to you-you will be released from my oath." Then they asked Rebekah, "Will you go with this man?" "I will go," she said. Genesis 24*

> *Rachel was lovely in form, and beautiful. Jacob was in love with Rachel. Genesis 29:17-18*

> *The Lord God said, "It is not good for the man to be alone. I will make a helper suitable for him." Genesis 2:18*

Now your life is changing and you feel you are ready to date for marriage. Dating for marriage is different than dating just to hang out and have company. Dating for marriage means that whoever you go out with is a more serious candidate for a lifelong commitment. When you date for marriage you are more serious-minded. You should also be highly discerning at this stage. You should have skills of accepting and refusing people from practice you gained as a teenager. You will ultimately only choose one person and refuse all others, so hopefully by now your refusal skills are razor sharp. At this stage you are looking for the one and the only who will fit into the vision that the Lord has given you for your life. You should know more at this point then you knew previously. If you are surer about your life's work, then your spouse should definitely be a match regarding whether or not their aspirations can morph with yours. Someone determined to live in the same city they grew up in cannot marry a missionary or a military man who will move often. If they are determined to remain stationary and they marry a military man, then they set themselves up for certain conflict, which could be avoided with careful thought, prayer, and wisdom from older Christians.

Once you have several candidates of people that will fit into your life, then you can choose based on preferences like close proximity to your hometown to make seeing extended family easier, chemistry and physical attraction, and of course personality. It is essential that both parties in a Christian marriage consent to the marriage, and it is also important that the parents of the bride and groom find the spouse a desirable match for their adult child. This is not a law, as there are always exceptions, but it is a guideline. If your parent is strongly opposed it would be wise to hear them out and to consider carefully the reasons for their disapproval.

Once you are seriously dating and you expect to propose or expect a proposal, then please work to keep your engagement time as brief as possible. A brief engagement provides for less sexual temptation and I desire that you stay innocent until your wedding day.

Love is important and love will grow over time. A love marriage is a wonderful gift from God and should be celebrated, but try to remember the marriage is more important than the party. Last of all, as with any binding oath where you are giving your word, your promise, inquire of the Lord, Lord may I marry this individual? Seek the Lord. Make certain you ask if you have His approval as well as the approval of the parents of the bride to be.

Further Study: Genesis 2, Genesis 24, Ex 22:16-17 Mark 10, Ephesians 5, 1 Corinthians 11

Marriage, Divorce, Fidelity, Guard Your Heart
Dating and Sexuality

> *Marriage should be honored by all. Hebrews 13:4*
>
> *Each man should have his own wife, and each woman her own husband...each man has his own gift from God. 1Corinthians 7*
>
> *Guard yourself in your spirit and do not break faith with the wife of your youth. "I hate divorce." Malachi 2:16*
>
> *Above all else, guard your heart, for everything you do flows from it. Proverbs 4:23*

Dear Ones, God approves of marriage as a means to decrease loneliness in our lives. Some people are given the gift of singleness and some are given the gift of marriage. God allows both and blesses both. Marriage should be honored means that marriage is a good thing and shouldn't be looked down upon in any way. God created it and He is for it. But God does stipulate in His word that it be between a man and a woman. God desires to bless His people with physical children. To have a child requires an egg and a sperm. God desires to bless people with offspring that delight the human heart. God doesn't want anyone to miss out on this great gift and that is one of the most important reasons for the rule for heterosexual marriage.

Dear friends, with kindness I share these important words for you. Divorce is not God's best. I tell you these things out of love. I do not condemn those who have already divorced, but I want to keep you from divorcing in the future. Divorce is preventable in most cases and I want to help keep you from getting divorced. Knowing that divorce breaks God's heart is motivation for you to stay faithful when you are married some day. This is so important because human sexuality is a powerful gift. Sex is like the super glue that holds two people together. Your heart is intricately intertwined with what you do with your body. If you give yourself to someone sexually, then your heart becomes wrapped up in that person. When you then break that bond, your heart experiences brokenness that is extremely painful and I desire to keep you from that pain. I have heard it said that breaking up with someone after having had a sexual relationship with that person is equal to experiencing the loss of death. It hurts and it hurts badly. This is what I want to keep you from. So when you don't give yourself to people sexually outside of marriage, and instead save yourself sexually until marriage, then you are taking good care of yourself. You are guarding not only your body, but you are guarding your heart from excruciating, unnecessary pain. Abstinence provides for protection not only from pregnancy and sexually transmitted diseases but also provides protection from emotionally wrenching break-ups.

For Further Study: Matthew 5, 1Corinthians 7, Matthew 19, Proverbs 5

Jesus Is God-Kingdom Takeoff or Takeover?
Understanding Jesus

> *The Son is the radiance of God's glory, the exact representation of his being, sustaining all things by his powerful word. After he had provided for purification of sins he sat down at the right hand of the Majesty in heaven. Hebrews 1:3*
>
> *"I and the Father are one." John 10:30 (Jesus)*
>
> *They all asked, "Are you then, the Son of God?"*
>
> *He replied, "You are right in saying I am." Luke 22:70 (Jesus)*

Who is Jesus? Is he a prophet or just a teacher, or is Jesus the Son of God, part of the trinity? Jesus was crucified because he claimed to be God. Jesus suffered and died because of who He said He was. This is central because Jesus was not killed because He was a murderer or a thief. He was killed for theological reasons. He was killed because of His power and because He had a huge following and there was fear that His following would continue to grow and take over the religious power structure that was in place at that time. The religious power structure was trying to prevent a takeover, a coup so to speak.

People vie for power and fight for power. Jesus was viewed as a threat to the power structure of his day and that is the reason He was opposed. Jesus did talk repeatedly about the kingdom of God. Many Jews wanted God to fully establish his kingdom at that time, but interestingly God chose us and wants us to partner with Him to bring His kingdom fully to the world. God doesn't want to do it alone. The Jews went to Pilate and asked for Jesus to be crucified, because the Jews did not want to be blamed for Jesus' death. Pilate wanted to release Jesus, but it was the Jewish religious leadership who feared a takeover that would disrupt their power because many Jews were coming to Christ. In the midst of this turmoil, Jesus began a New Covenant, one that required the shedding of blood, which allowed for the Gospel to then takeoff and spread throughout the earth.

So, yes, Jesus is God and one of the three persons of the trinity. The three in one is a great mystery. God is one essence but three distinct persons. The mystery of Jesus being the exact representation of God is indeed mesmerizing and fascinating to contemplate. Yet the Scriptures plainly teach this concept.

Jesus' Gospel takeoff would eventually prepare for a takeover of the entire earth where earth and heaven will be reconciled together, but that day has not yet come. Jesus began the New Covenant that replaced the Old Covenant. Jesus started a new movement, merging Jews and Gentiles together. Some Jews stayed Jews, however some Jews believed in Jesus and together with believing Gentiles became known as Christians.

Further Study: Genesis 15, Genesis 17, Jeremiah 31:31, Luke 8:1, John 3:1-21, Hebrews 8:8-13, Hebrew 12:24

Special thanks to N.T. Wright

Jesus Is Not A Password-Be A Disciple
Understanding Jesus

> *"Not everyone who says to me, 'Lord, Lord,' will enter the kingdom of heaven, but only the one who does the will of my Father who is in heaven. Matthew 7:21*

My son David occasionally speaks to me in what I call Dave Phrase. David is always ready to put the truths of God into our culture in order to help us to think contemporarily what Jesus means today in our culture. When David says Jesus is not a password he means this—it takes more than covering your bases by saying the prayer of faith as a child, "Jesus come into my heart" while inwardly thinking, Oh, I'm glad I have that done now. I've got my ticket to heaven, let me move on now and get about my life. The prophet Jeremiah put it this way, "Long ago you broke off your yoke and tore off your bonds; you said, "I will not serve you"

(Jer. 2:20). God knows our heart. He desires us to be deeply engaged with Him and caught up in a lifestyle of following Him. God knows if we pray the sinner's prayer and don't really invite Jesus into our life but instead only check a box. Do not be deceived, checking a box is not inviting God into your life. No, rather inviting God into your life is saying I am off the throne of doing things my way and I am putting myself under the master teacher, Jesus, and I am becoming a Christ follower. You see Jesus did really live a masterful life. Jesus mastered all of life's challenges. Jesus did not reply in hatred when others were hateful toward Him. Jesus stopped and helped others even when they were crowding around Him and He was exhausted. Jesus was not arrogant but freely welcomed children and the seemingly unimportant people into his circle of friendships. Jesus mastered life and therefore He is our general, our teacher, our master and is worthy of being followed. Jesus is not a password into heaven. Rather Jesus is heaven to all of us who refuse to just let him pass by us without becoming our all and all.

If you are trying to embrace the world and have Jesus on the side—indeed if you treat Jesus as though he is just a password, then take warning. Dear friend, Jesus wants to be the main dish, he is not content to be the side dish. You believe that there is one God. Good! Even the demons believe that—and shudder. Maybe some of us took Jesus as our savior as a child, but as we grow and mature we might need to renew that commitment as we begin to understand what it really means to follow Jesus. As we grow up we realize Jesus is not a password, He is our master teacher who is trustworthy for all of the questions of our hearts. I testify to you He is my best friend and is deeply reliable. Yes, put your trust in Him for salvation, but He must also be Lord and master of your life.

Further Study: Luke 5:27, Luke 9:23, Luke 9:59, Luke 14:27, Luke 18:22, Matthew 3:7-10

Special Thanks to David Swarbrick, Jr. for creating the saying, "Jesus is not a password".

Jesus Takes the Blow-Atonement

Understanding Jesus

> *They put a purple robe on him, then twisted together a crown of thorns and set it on him....They put a staff in his right hand. Then they knelt in front of him and mocked him. "Hail, king of the Jews!" they said. Matt 27:29, Mark 15:17*

Jesus is the fall guy. He always takes the fall. Jesus is the lover of my soul. He walks with me in the cool of the morning and in the brilliance of the day. He knows my ways and sends me little messages that He is watching me. He comforts me with His rod of correction and I fall down on bended knee with a grateful acknowledgment of his kind discipline. Who would think that He would consider my moments and offer me the rich wisdom of His kind rebuke that I might grow and improve! How gracious He is. After He knows my ways and hits me with the rod of correction, He moves on swiftly ahead of me.

He races on ahead. I wonder what He is up to? What can the Blessed One be doing? Then I catch a glimpse. He is on ahead with the accuser. The evil one is bludgeoning Jesus with blows. The blows are the stripes due me for my failings, for my real rebellion, for my flat out denials of Christ, for my lack of wanting to be identified with Jesus.

I catch up to Him now, and I see He has taken my blows for me. He has thrown himself under the bus for me. My debt has been paid for on the cross. The accuser is gone and The Blessed One carries my shame. Relief swells my soul like a flood. Water cleanses me. I am so relieved to not carry the full brunt—the full consequence of my choices. I was despondent considering all that I really deserved. Yet now I am free. I still suffer some but not as much. The Precious One embraces me in His arms. He welcomes me. He has taken my blows. He has lessened my penalty. He has healed my diseases. He has restored my spirit.

Jesus, You are my atonement.

You have taken my blows.

I fall down on bended knee

And acknowledge you are the Christ

You are the Messiah

You are the Promised One

I have been waiting for.

Further Study: John 1:29, Romans 5:12-21, Romans 6:10, Hebrews 9:26-28

Special Thanks to Pastor Jake Lindsey

Jesus is Our High Priest-What To Do When We Are Muddy
Understanding Jesus

> *...We have a high priest who has ascended into heaven...For we do not have a high priest who is unable to empathize with our weaknesses, but we have one who has been tempted in every way, just as we are-yet he did not sin. Let us then approach God's throne of grace with confidence, so that we may receive mercy and find grace to help us in our time of need. Hebrews 4:14-16*
>
> *If we confess our sins, he is faithful and just and will forgive us our sins and purify us from all unrighteousness. 1John 1:9*

So we have an idea of priesthood. We understand that a priest prays for us, on behalf of us. But now Jesus has come and Jesus has appeared once for all at the culmination of the ages, to do away with sin by sacrificing Himself (Heb 9:26). Jesus has become the one we can go directly to with our soul work. So the first step is to go to Jesus when we sin, when our souls get muddy by our earthly lives. We all fall short in various ways and at times fall into sin unintentionally and get muddied up. At those points we need to confess our sins to Jesus. Jesus already knows what we have done, however, cleansing comes when we confess. To confess means merely to agree with God about the truth. If I have taken the last donut and have blamed it on my brother then my soul has been muddied because I have lied. Now it might not seem profitable to confess to your parent that you have taken the last donut, however if you do confess it to both Jesus and your parent, then you will receive the wonderful reward of a clean conscience, regardless of any punishment you receive or don't receive. The most important thing is to bring your sins to Jesus as your priest.

Now the second point to learn from Jesus is how to keep moving forward in grace. When we sin we often feel bad. However the truth is being in right standing with God is not a feeling, but a fact based on God's promise to purify us. God is willing to help us move forward after we have confessed and been cleansed. He longs for us to come to Him and receive grace. We go forward, forgetting the past sin, resolving to not practice sin, to keep learning from the Master.

Jesus understands us because He came to earth and felt what it was like to be tempted. Because He came to earth He understands our weaknesses. Jesus knows how to help us overcome temptation because He, unlike us, was sinless and perfectly overcame temptation at every challenge He faced. Because of that, He eagerly awaits to bestow on us grace to continue on in our journey of following Him. When we became a Christian we received atonement and forgiveness of sin. Additionally, we also have Jesus who intercedes for us as our High Priest (Hebrews 7:25).

Further Study: Hebrews 4-10, 1 Timothy 2:5-6

No Condemnation-You Are Not A Punching Bag
Understanding Jesus

> *Therefore there is no condemnation for those who are in Christ Jesus, because through Christ Jesus, the law of the Spirit who gives life, has set you free from the law of sin and death. Romans 8:1,2*
>
> *In addition to all this, take up the shield of faith, with which you can extinguish all the flaming arrows of the evil one. Ephesians 6:16*

This truth must be read over and over until it sinks in. If necessary, read it out loud, yes, even shout it to yourself until it sinks in. Many Christians need to be reminded of this great truth of Scripture periodically throughout their lives. Jesus does not give us salvation, forgiveness, healing, and hope just to leave us condemned. No rather Jesus truly removes the condemnation that was ours before Jesus saved us. In some ways it is like when you build a new house and move in. Everything is now different. Newness has come to you because you now live in God's house. You have been made new. You are now in God's family. You are a saint now, you no longer live in the house of sin. Yes, you sometimes still sin, but now you belong to God. You have passed from death to life and you are now a part of the house of God.

If you are a part of God's house then you should not be beating yourself up. You are not a punching bag, you do not need to receive blow after blow after blow. Yes you need to turn from sin, yes there are some things you need to stop doing. Yes you must renounce sinful and shameful ways and repent. But Jesus now is alive in you and He is the goodness of God in you. This is what being good is: it is believing in Jesus and allowing Jesus to reign in your body. Once we were dead in our sins and no goodness resided in us. But now Christ has come in by faith and now goodness reigns in us. Sometimes we will lose battles against sin. If we do sin, we can make a personal confession to the Father and we will receive grace and forgiveness. We received forgiveness when we first became a Christian, but then we still need daily grace as we live out our lives of faith before God. Being in God's house means we have the protection of God's Son, Jesus. Jesus bore our sins at Calvary, which means that Jesus is now like the defender who is on our side. People who want to take you on and condemn you, now have to face Jesus first. Jesus is your defender. When we sin, and the evil one wants to make a big deal about it, he has to take it up with Jesus. The thing is Jesus already died on your behalf, Jesus knows you are counting on Him. Jesus is your defender. He has taken up your case (Lamentations 3:58).

Discernment comes with time. In time you will be able to recognize the evil one's voice as the accuser who wants to keep you defeated, the one who wants you to believe you are condemned. In time you will be able to recognize the voice of Jesus. It is the voice of Jesus who says there is no condemnation for those in Christ Jesus. Instead, there is confession, repentance and turning our backs on sin. If it is our heart to become more like Christ, to turn from sin, then we don't need to treat ourselves like we are just a punching bag that receives blows, instead we can rebuke those blows, put up our shield against those blows and rest that we are in the household of God and Jesus will defend us.

Further Study: Ephesians 6:10-20, 2Corinthians 5:1

You've Got Family-Close or Distant Relative?
Understanding Jesus

> *He predestined us for adoption for sonship through Jesus Christ, in accordance with his pleasure and will. Ephesians 1:5*
>
> *Now Jesus' mother and brothers came to see him... He replied, "My mother and brothers are those who hear God's word and put it into practice." Luke 8:19-21*

Dear Ones, some of us have lost parents through tragic deaths. If this is your case, I am sorry for your loss. God's heart breaks for the situation that orphans the world over face. A great truth is that God's desire is that those who do not have physical parents be carefully looked after on earth. God's desire is that the Christian community will care for those who do not have parents. If you find yourself in this situation, I pray you find some comfort knowing that adoption is a principle that every Christian must wrestle with whether or not they have physical parents living. God fathers all of His Christian children, some of whom are blessed to also be parented by earthly fathers. God is our Father and we are his sons and daughters.

This is a privileged position, how did we get to be sons and daughters in God's family? We have been selected and we have not been rejected. Celebrate, Hallelujah, we've all been adopted by God and predestined for sonship. Predestined means planned. So God planned for our adoption for sonship ahead of time before Jesus actually came. It is similar to adoption of any child today. One does not say today I want a child let's go pick one up. No it requires planning and interviews and house visits and legal documents. In the same way, God planned for our adoption into His family by utilizing Jesus in order to get us adopted. This was a costly endeavor on God's part to sacrifice His own son so that we could be adopted into His family, but the Scripture says that not only was it God's will to do that, but it gave Him pleasure to do it. God was pleased to make a way for us. In a similar way people who work in adoption offices are pleased to make a way for people to have a child who otherwise are unable to do so.

Dear Ones, I do not want you to be unaware that being in Jesus' family means that we have a certain destiny. Our destiny as children of God is to become more and more like Jesus. When you have physical parents, you physically look like your parents, similarly when you have God as your parent, you should look like God and reflect God's glory.

Now, I do not want you to be unaware that Jesus had actual physical brothers. But when this point was called on for discussion, Jesus turned it aside in order to focus on the most important truth about family which was that the closest ones to Jesus were those who actually practiced what they preached. This is key to understanding the heart of who Jesus is. Jesus is not about hypocrisy-He is not about words. Jesus rather is about practice. To practice something means to work at getting better at it. Jesus is blessed by those who hear God's word and keep incorporating it into their life practices. God is not blessed so much by the Bible scholar, God is blessed by the Bible doer. So the closest ones to God, the closest family members are the Bible doers. Are you a close relative, or distant? Have you remembered to do the word?

Further Study: Matthew 5,6,7; 1Timothy 4:16; James 1:22-27

Redeemer, Valuable Coupon

Understanding Jesus

> *The Redeemer will come to Zion, to those in Jacob who repent of their sins declares the Lord. Isaiah 59:20*
>
> *And who is like your people Israel-the one nation on earth that God went out to redeem as a people for himself, and to...perform great and awesome wonders by driving out nations and their gods from before your people, whom you redeemed from Egypt? 2Samuel 7:23*
>
> *But God will redeem me from the realm of the dead; he will surely take me to himself. Psalm 49:15*

Dear Ones, coupons in and of themselves have no value. If you try to get cash for a coupon you would not be able to get cash. On most paper coupons it says in tiny print something like 1/64 cents. The value of the paper is a very, very small amount, in most cases less than a penny. However, when the coupon is redeemed, there is added value. The value of the coupon suddenly could go as high as 50 cents, a dollar, or even ten dollars. In the same way that a coupon receives added value, so too, when we are redeemed we move into the added value arena. Our redemption puts us in the place of value.

God can redeem any life and make any life new for anyone who truly repents. If someone's life has been marked by abysmal failure, that life can be redeemed. What in the world do I mean by that? Redemption means to add value to what originally looks only hopeless and worthless. Jesus is our Redeemer who has rescued us from sin and separation from God and purifies us and leads us to live lives that please God the Father. Anyone's life that has been a complete failure can come to Jesus and begin anew. I tell you a mystery-God can add value to those things that seem valueless. It's like this-if you surrender your life to God and truly are sold out to Him, then God can take your previous broken relationships, your previous misdeeds and begin to breathe life into broken ways. He can use you to bring forgiveness and reconciliation. As you repent then He can lead the way back to being restored to others. Jesus can add value to what in the past looked hopeless. He can restore broken relationships, He can repair what you messed up, He can use you as an instrument of reconciliation in the world. As you become like the redeemer, then you become an instrument that aides others towards redemption. God does not want to give you pain, He wants to give you value added purpose-He wants to add value to what you've suffered, and make it useful.

Further Study: Leviticus 25,26,27;Luke 24:21; Galatians 3:13; 4:5, Titus 2:14

I've Got You Covered
Understanding Jesus

> *For while we are in this tent, we groan and are burdened, because we do not wish to be unclothed but to be clothed instead with our heavenly dwelling so that what is mortal may be swallowed up by life....Therefore we are always confident and know that as long as we are at home in the body we are away from the Lord. So we make it our goal to please him. 2Corinthians 5:2,4,9*
>
> *But we know that when Christ appears, we shall be like him, for we shall see him as he is. 1John 3:2*

Dear Ones, not many of us have been caught naked, but if this has happened to you, it probably brought feelings of embarrassment. It would be uncomfortable to be the only naked person in a room, or to be dressed in gym clothes at a banquet. To have clothes is necessary and to wear appropriate attire for certain occasions is culturally respectful. One could actually die as a result of not having proper clothing in extremely cold climates such as the Alaskan winter, or in an extremely hot climate such as the Sahara desert. Clothes cover in order to preserve life, but also to allow life to go on without distraction.

Being spiritually clothed has some similarities to being physically clothed. Jesus is our atonement. Jesus is our covering. As the Passover vividly portrays being covered by the blood of the lamb, so too, Jesus' death on the cross was an act which vividly provided covering, an atonement for sins. Atonement is a completed, finished work. As many of you that have been baptized into Christ, so too, you have put on Christ. Although the covering provided through the atoning work of Christ on the cross is a completed work, just as an oil painting is completely done, there still are paintings that come after that work, so to speak. Those of us who are in Christ are clothed with salvation. After we have been clothed in salvation, we then have access to other beautiful clothes. As we mature in Christ, we have the privilege of being clothed in the majesty of our God. Because the Spirit lives in us, we can be clothed with integrity and faithfulness, we can have a vibrant interior spiritual life, we can be clothed with compassion, kindness, humility, gentleness and patience. We should not be ones who are clothed in shame and violence. We have purpose.

Yet, Paul in 2Corinthians still is aware of the longing and the groaning of the unmet desire to be completely and utterly clothed in Christ. We have been given a deposit, the Spirit of God, which guarantees what is to come and we continue to walk by faith, clothing ourselves in Christ. The blood of the Lamb covers us and we are covered in the likeness of Christ and others can behold His glory in us. This is our identity; we are ones who are covered and therefore we may approach God with freedom and confidence. Yet, until we are clothed with our heavenly dwelling, we still experience a longing that is only partially fulfilled. But when Christ appears, we shall be like Him, for we shall see Him as He is. In that instant, we will be completely covered in the image of God. We are covered, we are being covered, and we will be completely covered.

Further Study: Gen 3:21, Gen 20:16, Ex 12, Ex 25:17-22, Ex 28, Ex 33:22, Job 40:10, Ps 91:4, Prov 31:21-22, Isa 11:9, Isa 61:10, Eze 9:2-3, Eze 23:6, Eze 32:1-14, Lk 24:49, Rom 13:14, 1Cor 15:51-54, 2Cor 5, Gal 3:27, Eph 1:1-2:10, Col 3:12, 1Pet 5:5, Rev 3:17-18

Who Are You Chillin' With?
Habits To Avoid

Do not be misled: "Bad company corrupts good character." 1 Corinthians 15:33

Dear Ones, if you keep hanging out with the shady people do you think that it doesn't matter? Do you think in your mind Jesus hung out with sinners, so I should too? Well one must look deeper to see what your motives are. Jesus hung out with sinners for the express goal of saving them. Is that your goal, or is it so you can join them in their sin? I heard another way of putting this, are your gloves getting muddy or are your friends getting glovvy? When you are growing up sometimes you just need to hang out with people who are stronger than you or friends who are trying to go in the same direction as you. It doesn't mean to have perfect friends because those don't exist. Friends are good because if they see their friend falling down they can offer a hand to lift them up. On the other hand if your friend is pulling you so far down that they are truly getting you into trouble then perhaps it is time to put an end to that friendship.

I heard a story once about a guy-we will call him Sam- who went cruising with his friend-we will call him Bill. Sam had no clue his friend Bill was about to go on a murderous rampage. Bill ended up killing several people. Sam drove the car that day without knowing what Bill was planning. Sam didn't find the strength to retreat from the event once the plan got set into motion and ended up with a fifteen year prison sentence for being in the wrong place and for hanging out with the wrong crowd. Don't be foolish in your thinking. As a young person it matters whom you are hanging out with. You have to be able to realize your strengths and your weaknesses. Now, we say in our heart, wow, Sam really had bad luck. But did he, or is it as though Sam kept choosing to be with Bill even though earlier in his heart of hearts he knew Bill was headed in the wrong direction? Usually there are clues, so listen to your intuition-and pray and ask God to help you decide if you should hang out with someone or not. God knows what is best for you. In addition, here is some wisdom for you. Ask yourself the following questions. Are you the leader in the friendship? Is someone following you because they want a wild life or are they following you because they want Jesus and because you epitomize a good, wholesome lifestyle? On the other hand are you the follower in the friendship? Are you following someone who is the leader in the friendship and are they exhibiting a good wholesome lifestyle, a life of following Jesus, or are you following them and they value debauchery and carousing and are bent on evil? It is one thing when someone is following you because they want to leave their current lifestyle and know Jesus, it is quite another when you are following someone who has no intentions of following Jesus. So sure, non-Christians can be in your group but they cannot be your group's leader. And yes, someone can lead you as long as they are strongly for Christ. Furthermore, if you are surrounding yourself with non-Christians, are you by yourself or is another Christian friend with you? See, what it really has to do with is what exactly is your motive? What are you going for?

When Jesus sent his disciples out to do mission how did He send them? Of course He sent them out two by two. If you are trying to rescue others and bring them into the kingdom, that is good, but don't do it alone. If possible do it prayerfully with a group of Christian friends.

Further Study: Prov16:25-30,.23:17-21; Psalm 101:4, Ephesians 5:11, 2Timothy 3:5, Titus 3:10

What's That You're Wearing?
Habits To Avoid

> *I also want the women to dress modestly, with decency and propriety, adorning themselves, not with elaborate hairstyles or gold or pearls or expensive clothes, but with good deeds, appropriate for women who profess to worship God. 1Timothy 2:9-10*

> *By smooth talk and flattery they deceive the minds of naïve people. Romans 16:18*

So of course, we all get a little annoyed when people are focusing so much on our clothes, but if we all dressed modestly then there would be nothing to say, what is the big deal anyway? Well the big deal is the way we are made. Men and women are made with an affinity, an attraction for one another. There is something about a young athletic body that is mesmerizing when it is scantily clothed. Men are primarily moved to the place of sin via the eye, women are moved to the place of sin via the ear, although both can succumb to the eye or the ear. Just as women should not be scantily clothed, so men should not seduce naïve women with smooth talk.

Unbridled seduction by women and untenable promises by men should both be avoided. It can be especially uncomfortable when a young teenager wears inappropriate clothes to church events. This can be embarrassing for the faith community who is trying to focus on the Lord, but finds a young woman to be distracting. The truth is sometimes we all make mistakes and as young women, mistakes in dress is something all of us have done. As boys and young men, we have made mistakes in our smooth talking. There's a tension there, because God has made woman and has made her to be attractive and pleasing to the eye, and God has made men to invite a women for marriage. God calls us to modesty in our dress, and God calls us to have integrity of speech. God does not want us to cause our brothers or sisters to stumble.

Equally, we should all commit ourselves to dress modestly and to speak circumspectly. And for some of us, that is our issue, we figure if others are doing it, what really is the difference? We reason within ourselves that we need attention. Our interior motive might be our need to get attention and to get looked at. We often dress or speak with the motive of being noticed. We have to ask ourselves, what are we going for? We should be hoping that others see Christ in us, instead of hoping others focus on what our body looks like. We want to be the Lord's friend and we want to attract members of the opposite sex who also want to be the Lord's friend. Please be careful with how you dress and how you speak.

Further Study: Job 40:10, Isaiah 51:9, Is 52:1, Ephesians 6:10-18, Col 3:6-14, 1Thess 2:5

What's That You're Saying? Fresh Cheese and Moldy Bread?

Habits To Avoid

Do not let any unwholesome talk come out of your mouths, but only what is helpful for building others up. Ephesians 4:29

Rejoice with those who rejoice, mourn with those who mourn. Romans 12:15

Out of the same mouth come praise and cursing. My brothers and sisters this should not be. James 3:10

Dear friends, we've all been around people who curse and criticize other people and we want better things for these people. There is a better way than speaking out against others with criticism and gossip. If this is a habit that is besetting you, then take heart there is hope. Maybe you've gotten into a bit of a bad habit with your mouth. If you have, then the first thing to do is to admit it and to ask the Lord to help you to use your mouth to bless, not to curse. If you struggle to use your mouth to bless others it is possibly because you yourself have been the recipient of curses. If this is the case, then you need to be healed from evil words spoken over you. After you have asked the Lord for help in this area, then the second step is to not believe lies that have been spoken over you. If you are in Christ, then you are a new creature and that is your identity-you are a child of a king and deeply loved. Because God loves you, He wants to give you a new mindset. His mindset is that you are part of His dignified family, and as a dignified one, you don't receive evil words spoken over you.

The third step is to deal with any unhealed hurts in your heart that lead you to curse or criticize or gossip about others. To deal with hurts, you must admit hurt resides in your heart, and be open to receive healing from God.

Finally, we become better at things we practice at, so start practicing not cursing others and practice blessing others instead. When my kids were little, if I caught them saying bad things about their siblings, I would take them aside and make them give three or more compliments to make up for every slur that they hurled against their sibling. I have to admit some of their compliments were pretty weak, you know they'd say things like, "I really like your blond hair", or "I like your skinny legs". But I encouraged them to give true compliments and to practice saying things that honored their siblings and they got the point and they got better at blessing with practice. So, as with anything worth doing, practice and you will improve. Restrain your tongue from speaking evil over others. It is best to keep things that you know about people under your hat and not to go around gossiping, even if the information is true, keep it under your hat. In addition to practice not saying negative things, also practice saying things like, "I'm glad you're in my life, I like how kind you are to others, or I like how you love God." Because remember if you make a sandwich out of fresh cheese and moldy bread, well it's just not good. We want good words without any criticism and without any cursing, like a good cheese sandwich made with fresh bread.

Further Study: Matthew 12:36-37, James 1:19-27, James 3:1-12, James 4:13-17, 1Timothy 3:11, 1 Timothy 6:4, 3 John 1:10

What If I'm A Little Mad? You're Not The Tin Man
Habits To Avoid

Blessed are those who mourn, for they will be comforted. Matthew 5:4

Everyone should be quick to listen, slow to speak and slow to become angry, because human anger does not produce the righteousness that God desires. James 1:19-20

Dear friends, sometimes we have a tendency to make matters worse. Do you know what I mean? Some of us are in a bad situation already, and it may seem like no one cares and no one understands. We might be somewhat desperate for someone to understand us and we might even throw a temper tantrum in our desperation. Angry outbursts make things worse. Understanding anger can help us to overcome being angry.

Anger can come in many forms. Anger can sometimes just be an outburst that surprises with its intensity. Anger can also be more intentional and include hateful gossip where lies and falsehoods are spread about people out of jealousy. Anger can also almost feel like an illness that plagues you, that you want to get rid of, if you could only figure out what you are mad about! Anger might express itself in blaming other people for our situation. Anger can grow due to mounting personal frustration. Anger can be pushed down over a prolonged time and can turn into depression and even move to the point of becoming suicidal. (If you are suicidal, seek help immediately. Focus on the Family has free help at 1-855-771-HELP (4357)).

Dear friend, if you are struggling with anger, take heart, you are not alone in your struggle. What is one to do? In general it makes people uncomfortable to be around anger. If we get angry and we blow up, people won't come near us and we become even more isolated. The funny thing is when we get to that point we feel like it's not our fault. We feel victimized. It started with frustration and it all ends up snowballing into an even bigger mess.

I don't want this for you. This is what you have to do. You have to deal with the frustration first—deal with the situation you are avoiding. Journal about your situation, talk deeply about it to your youth leader or other Christian leader. Pray, and seek comfort from the Lord. Find your help in the Lord. Stop acting like you're not mad. Stop pretending like you're not hurt. You are hurt and that is okay. If you weren't hurt then you would be a robot. You would be the Tin Man. You are not the Tin Man. God did not make you without a heart. Hearts get hurt and that's okay. What's not okay is to not seek the Lord for help. What's not okay is to not tell others how hurt you've been. The body of Christ is to be a present help for ones who have been wounded by evil. If you do not tell anyone your situation, then you will not be able to heal. The people of God should help carry your burden.

Sometimes I would cry and I didn't know exactly what I was crying about. With friends I found it safer to be angry then to go to my heart. My heart seemed too complicated and I didn't understand my heart. It felt too messed up. I love the lyrics of a popular song that says plainly, "I've got a busted heart" (Musixmatch). I felt that for years. The truth is that many people face the truth of their busted hearts and get healing and help for deep wounds to be healed and their hearts get to a better place with the care of the Lord and the Lord's people. The good news is that the Lord can heal your broken heart. He has healed mine and I love Him for it. He can heal your heart also, but you must commit to doing the hard work of mourning your losses. Mourn well, but then also thank God that you are not a heartless Tin Man who feels nothing. Bless the Lord that you have a heart, and that the Lord is able to give you a heart of flesh. Refuse to be the Tin Man, content with a stony or bitter heart. Seek the Lord for a heart made of flesh. Ask the Lord to take away your anger and make sure you get some exercise, exercise helps to dissipate angry feelings.

Further Study: Job 5:11, Ezekiel 11:19, Ezekiel 36:26

Body Image Obsession-Character or Caricature?
Habits To Avoid

> *Do you not know that your bodies are temples of the Holy Spirit. You are not your own; you were bought at a price. Therefore honor God with your bodies. 1Corinthians 6:20*
>
> *For physical training is of some value, but godliness has value for all things. 1Timothy 4:8*
>
> *But godliness with contentment is great gain. 1Timothy 6:6*

So we've all been to a state fair where they have a boardwalk with vendors. Oftentimes these vendors at fairs include artists who draw funny caricatures of people. Now a caricature is simply a drawing with extreme facial or body features that are distorted. Most of the times when we see these distortions we laugh at the artist's skill at making fun of our facial or body features and we can take it as a joke. Yet for some of us, certain parts of our physical appearance are painful, especially for teens going through puberty. Teens can be upset over a myriad number of things such as hair color, height, weight, acne, etc. On some level emerging adults might not only have difficulty accepting perceived imperfections, but also when there is an actual social stigma or making a caricature out of one's physical appearance, it is almost too difficult for most teens to bear. Dear ones, you as young Christians must lead your peers by having strong character and not joining in on making caricatures out of peers who have bodily imperfections. Furthermore, leadership is needed to value people's character growth and development. If you are dishonoring someone because of his size or height then you are not being kind. People who are obsessed with the minor imperfections in a human body, especially having to do with their perceived notions of perfect beauty, are not honoring God the creator in the way they should.

Our culture is obsessed with body image and there is immense pressure on both young men and young women, but especially on young women; to have the perfect body and perfectly clear skin. But what do you do if you don't have that perfect body, maybe you're a little bigger boned than many of the other girls your age, or maybe you're a guy and you haven't had your growth spurt yet and the other males are pushing you around. Teens growing in their faith with the Lord desire to be kind, but sometimes miss the mark. Please listen dear friends, our culture is off track, our culture has an overemphasis on what our bodies look like and an under emphasis on what our characters look like. We need to stop judging on mere appearances. Being physically fit has a little value, but godliness is extremely valuable.

Now please ask yourself if you have an unhealthy obsession. If you are spending an inordinate amount of time working out, or worse, starving yourself or binging and purging, then please get some help. Learn instead to eat a healthy diet and get a healthy amount of exercise and develop and grow as a person and as a friend. Develop your gifts. All people are made in the image of God. Those of you who struggle with your weight, or your height, or your perceived lack of beauty; please remember your body is the temple of the Holy Spirit, and you want to glorify the Lord with your body. Use that as your motivation to shape up, get fit and eat healthier. Set a realistic goal, not to be perfect, but rather to be godly in how you take care of your body, which is a gift from God. Then live with what you've been given, do the best you can, and glorify the Lord! He loves you! You are fearfully and wonderfully made!

Further Study: 1 Timothy 4, 1 Timothy 6

What Are You Looking At?
Stay Off the Slip and Slide
Habits To Avoid

> *Your eye is the lamp of your body. When your eyes are healthy, your whole body also is full of light. But when they are unhealthy, your body also is full of darkness. Luke 11:34 (Jesus)*
>
> *I am the light of the world. John 8:12 (Jesus)*
>
> *What no eye has seen, what no ear has heard, and what no human mind has conceived-the things God has prepared for those who love him. 1Cor 2:9*

Dear friends, the Lord has wonderful things for us to see in the future. God has wondrous things planned for His friends. It is so important that you understand that there are good things for those who can delay gratification and wait on God and obey God. The important thing to do in life is to make sure you are good friends with God.

To be a good friend of God means to value what God values. One of the biggest things God values is light. God says that when your eyes are healthy then your whole body is full of light. God wants you to have healthy eyes. What does this mean, do I need to take some of those old people's eye vitamins? God is not talking about vitamins, God is talking about having vital signs, and he's talking about having vitality. Vitality means life. God wants you to always have life signs in your body. God wants light to fill your body so that you will be a life giving presence in all you do. In order to become this person you must be making correct choices and being careful little eyes what you see.

Listen, without going into detail, we know the deeds of darkness, we know the things that we are not supposed to be looking at. The idea you need to remember is simple. Looking at one inappropriate picture is a slip, but where unchecked slips continue, they can quickly escalate into a major downhill slide. Do not get on the slip and slide of being addicted to inappropriate images. If you are addicted to inappropriate images then you need to stop looking at those images. You must take steps to get help. Inappropriate pictures get seared on your brain and they breed unrealistic expectations of what real bodies look like. They breed discontent and they are a counterfeit to an actual relationship with a real person. My prayer for you is that you can get help to stop filling your body with darkness. It may seem harmless until you are addicted and you do not have the willpower to stop. What begins as an innocent glance, can become an overpowering stifling addiction, which could last a lifetime and result in broken relationships. Instead, keep your eyes on the Lord, doing so fills you with light. Stay off the slip and slide.

Further Study: 2Samuel 11,12; Matthew 5:27-30; Luke 11:34-36; John 1; John 3; Romans 1:27; Colossians 3:5; 1 Thessalonians 4:5; 1 Peter 4:3; 1 John 2:16

No Cutting, Don't Hurt Yourself
Habits To Avoid

> *Do you not know that you yourselves are God's temple and that God's Spirit dwells in your midst? If anyone destroys God's temple, God will destroy that person; for God's temple is sacred, and you together are that temple.*
> *1Corinthians 3:16-17*
>
> *Do not practice divination, or seek omens. Do not cut your bodies for the dead. I am the Lord. Leviticus 19:26-28*

Dear friend, if you have invited Jesus into your heart, then indeed God lives in you and you are a new creation. Your body is a temple and the Holy Spirit resides in you. And so this temple, this body we have must be dealt with respectfully, we must honor God with our bodies. The Scriptures state we must not cut the body because in a way we are giving in to the culture of death instead of the culture of life. Among young people who are dealing with difficult challenges I see an increase in cutting and it seems to me to be a cry to say, hey something is wrong. And so I agree, yes something is wrong! If you sense that something is wrong in the world you are correct. Things are not going like God planned for goodness and for people to be thriving in the Lord in the world. When you say you see things and they are wrong you are correct, however when you give in and cut yourself you are giving in to the dark side of things and you are going the wrong way. I have faith for you, but cutting shows you are struggling. God is always present to help you. Cry out to Him. He knows what you are facing. He is available to rescue you, to give you wisdom and strength to face the challenges of your life.

If you are at the place where you are cutting, drinking excessively, doing drugs, or getting in cars with people who drive recklessly or drive drunk; then I urge you in the Lord to seek the elders in your church to pray for you. If you are not comfortable going to the elders, then go to others who are spiritual and who are gifted in prayer and who have been walking with the Lord for years to help you out by praying for you. Many times dangerous behavior is entered into for multiple reasons that can be helped with prayer. You should not be a participant in dangerous behavior, and you should know that there are mature disciples in the body of Christ who will pray for you and not condemn you. The body of Christ is able to assist. You are loved and you are worthy of receiving help and encouragement. Do not continue in isolation. Focus on the Family offers free Christian Counseling: 1-855-771-HELP (4357)

Further Study: 1 Corinthians 6:19-20, 2 Corinthians 5:6-10, Psalm 34:3, Romans 15:6, Ephesians 5:18

Community Life
Habits To Practice

Do not give up meeting together as some are in the habit of doing, but encourage one another- and all the more as you see the Day approaching. Hebrews 10:25

Dear Ones, it is important to be with the people of God. For many years I was very focused on winning people to Christ. My heart's desire was that many would know Jesus and be saved. This heart for evangelism was a good thing and a gift from God, but it took me many years until I began to understand the need for community life. When I married, then I began to understand life in community, because this was my husband's strength. After we were married for many years I realized we each had a different emphasis regarding the Christian life, we each emphasized different values. My husband was more concerned with the preservation of community, whereas I was more concerned with enlarging the community and calling others to follow Jesus.

It is not as though either emphasis was wrong, it was more that they were both right. An evangelist must call individuals to follow Jesus, but a community pastor calls Christians to join together to remain strong as a group so that they can work together to make disciples. The goals for the church must include both calling new people to follow Jesus as well as preserving the community life via discipleship. Both evangelism and community life-building disciples- are needed. The truth is, in the early church some of these same struggles occurred when the Gentiles were grafted into what was formerly a Jewish only religion and that's why there was some pushback.

But today we know that the Lord wants us to keep meeting together and finding life together in the family of God. The Lord wants us to pray together, share our lives together, and reach others with the message of Jesus' love and forgiveness. As we chill out together, love each other, and share our gifts, we will find that we are stronger and can do more as a group than we can do as single individuals. There's a saying, "The whole is greater than the sum of the parts" (Aristotle). What this means is that a synergy happens which is somewhat unexplainable when people work together, namely that interactions occur between people that can't be accounted for with a normal equation. Somehow if you normally add up the two hundred people in a fellowship and you add one hundred new converts you think you have a church of three hundred, but instead you end up with a church of five hundred. Now how did that happen? There's some group effect that occurs, some mobilization effect that wasn't planned on. As people find out about your love and good deeds, they want to know the Jesus you know who brings hope and deeply changes lives, they hear about your group and so they come! This is the synergy that can happen for communities who commit to work together as a community to share the Good News of Jesus.

Further Study: Acts 11:26, 28:15; 1Corinthians 11-16, Hebrews 10:24
Special Thanks to David Swarbrick, Sr. and Eric Swarbrick

Study The Word-It's A Treasure Trove
Habits To Practice

> *I have hidden your word in my heart that I might not sin against you. Your word is a lamp for my feet and a light for my path. Psalm 119:105, Psalm 119:111*
>
> *All Scripture is God-breathed and is useful for teaching, rebuking, correcting and training in righteousness. 2Timothy 3:16*

Imagine a basket next to your feet that is filled with hundred dollar bills. If you counted it all up, the trove of treasure would have a value of two million dollars. Would you use the money? Of course you would. You would probably pay for your education, buy a car, and buy a house. You would feel so rich, that you might even buy your parents a house or help them buy furniture. You would still have money left over after it was all said and done. In reality, the Bible is a book that is worth more than that basket of money yet so many people are not reading the book. The Bible is a great treasure trove and you will get so much joy if you read it.

Where should you start? It's important to understand that the Bible is divided into two sections-the Old Testament and the New Testament. The Old Testament contains the history of God from creation until the time of Christ. The New Testament tells the story of God from the time of Christ until the establishment of the early Church and foretells the future in the book of Revelation. I recommend you read the New Testament first to understand who Jesus is. Specifically I recommend you read the Gospel of Luke and the Gospel of John. Then after you've read that you can go to the Old Testament if you like and read the first book of the Old Testament, which is Genesis. You can also read some of the Psalms and Proverbs. The main thing is to understand who Jesus is and become a disciple of Jesus. Jesus is the main person to learn about. As you read the Gospels, try to write out verses that are specifically meaningful to you and memorize those that are meaningful to you. You should become disciplined in your study. Try to read at least twenty minutes for four or more days in every week. You don't want to be legalistic about it, but you do want to start a regular habit of reading the Bible. Why? You should read the Bible because the Bible helps you to know God. The Bible helps you to know how to live your life and is a resource filled with guidance to assist you. The Bible is there to keep you on track, it's there to encourage you when you get down, and it is a treasure trove in your walk with Jesus.

Further Study: Isaiah 55:11, Luke 8:1-15, Ephesians 6:17, Hebrews 4:12

Rocking Out to Christian Music
Habits To Practice

> *Then Miriam the prophetess, Aaron's sister, took a timbrel in her hand, and all the women followed her, with timbrels and dancing. Miriam sang to them, "Sing to the Lord for he is highly exalted. Both horse and driver he has hurled into the sea." Exodus 15:20-21*

Miriam is the first female prophetess mentioned in the Old Testament. Miriam was not only a prophetess, but she was also a worship leader. She was the sister of Moses and Aaron. Miriam led the Israelite women in singing and dancing after the Lord rescued them from the hand of Pharaoh and delivered the Israelites from slavery. The Israelites sang robustly as they saw the glory of God and witnessed His mighty power to deliver. The Israelites worshiped the

Lord freely. Before the Israelites were freed, Moses asked Pharaoh repeatedly to release the Israelites so that the Israelites could go and worship God. Finally in Exodus 12, Pharaoh releases all the Israelites to go out and worship the Lord. God desires to be worshiped and worship includes singing and praising the Lord. Jesus, in Luke 4, also refers to worship as the primary means to serve the Lord.

The Book of Psalms is a songbook and it is a record of songs sung before the time of Christ, but also today, many contemporary Christian artists have set many of the Psalms to music. We do not have ancient sheet music to go with the Psalms but we know that many of the Psalms were sung by the faith community.

But we wonder, is it important to sing and if so why? A big part of the why is simply that the Christian understands who God is and worship is simply agreeing with God. As we know God, we recognize His power, His kindness, His forgiveness, and His holiness. As we meditate on whom He is, our hearts do well up with praise and thanksgiving. And as we do, the Lord is blessed to hear us singing His praises and acknowledging whom God is to us who believe. Many of the Psalms, call the Christian to utilize musical instruments to help praise the Lord, or to shout with a loud voice. God is pleased when our souls magnify the Lord. Additionally, we find encouragement when we sing and focus on the Lord. Through fixing our hearts and minds on the Lord in worship we refresh and renew our spirits, which empowers us to do the Lord's work in the world. So make a loud raucous sound of praise to the Lord today, rock out in praise and adoration for Jesus.

Further Study: Exodus 1-15, Psalm 99:9, Psalm 149, Psalm 150, Isaiah 19:21, Luke 4:8
Special Thanks to my son, David Swarbrick, Jr.

Honor, Honor, Honor

Habits To Practice

Honor one another above yourselves. Romans 10b
The elders who direct the affairs of the church well are worthy of double honor, especially those whose work is preaching and teaching. 1Timothy 5:17

People in the Kingdom of God know how to give other people honor and how to submit to authority. A problem exists for people who have been wounded by ones in authority. When an authority figure greatly wounds someone who is not in power, then there is a tendency to rebel in order to survive.

If you are struggling with blessing those who are in authority over you it is okay. For right now, it is okay. What you must do is look deeper to the Lord to be your rescuer and deliverer. So God has been with you in the past, God is with you in the present, and God will be with you in the future if you have taken Him as your Lord and Savior. But as you grow in Him, He wants to redeem your past and teach you kingly behavior. Kings and queens, princes and princesses act well. An important element of good living is the willingness to give others honor and to subject one's self to authority.

The way to get better at honoring others is through practice. To put on the clothes of honor doesn't happen overnight. Don't be too hard on yourselves, but know that with practice, things get easier. What are some ways to practice showing honor? Simple things that you can do to show honor include: standing up when people enter the room, allowing others to go before you, greeting people when they enter the house-blessing them with a hug and a smile, calling people sir and ma'm and other kind words. You ask, "Well what do I do if my heart is not in it?" The point is to do it in obedience and eventually the heart of honor will follow.

Further Study Exodus 20:12, Numbers 20:12, Judges 13:17, 1Samuel 24, Luke 14:8, Romans 13:1-4, 1Corinthians 7:4, Jude 1:9

Special Thanks to Hope Chapel

Talk to the Lord Anytime, All the Time, Keep the Prayer Motor Running
Habits To Practice

> *Pray continually, give thanks in all circumstances; for this is God's will for you in Christ Jesus. Do not quench the Spirit. Do not treat prophesies with contempt; but test them all. 1Thessalonians 5:17-21*

When I was in college, I continued to spend time with Jesus and grew in being a disciple. I went to InterVarsity and Crusade meetings, led Bible studies, and hung out with those likeminded people who were eagerly following Jesus. Somewhere along the way these very dear people taught me how to have a quiet time. Spending time with Jesus was the path to spiritual renewal. We didn't always understand why we were doing certain things, but we just did them anyway because our leaders told us to do so. Many times I succeeded in having that quiet time. Many days I did not. I also heard about people who were spiritual masters who always had their quiet time and I was dismayed by my own lack of discipline.

Throughout the years I've kept a pretty consistent habit of meeting with the Lord. However if you look at my life, I am more the sprinter type rather than the marathoner. What I mean by this is, I am speedy and quick more so than slow and methodical. When I was young I also was mainly a producer. The thing I liked to do in the morning was to get after things, get things crossed off my list and get a good start on my day. The problem became that if I did that, then most assuredly I wouldn't have my quiet time and went the entire day without talking to Jesus. But Praise God that with time and practice I started to spend time with Jesus regularly. Now, even though I learned that it was a lie to believe that Jesus wasn't with me if I had not had my quiet time, I still had to work to discipline myself to do that which was most fruitful which was prioritizing spending time with the Lord in the morning before I started my day's work. Jesus' presence in my day does not depend on whether or not I have a quiet time, but my day was enhanced when I did have a quiet time. Even if I had not sat down quietly on a specific day, I still had the mind of Christ, I could still pray and seek the Lord and I could still access the Lord at any point throughout the day. We can pray and praise God while driving, while showering, while doing mundane chores around the house or in the yard. In fact, having mundane chores oftentimes allows for the heart and mind to focus on the Father, to have a spirituality that is alive and vibrant. But pray continually means of course that we are always on with God, we are always talking to Him, He is always with us and a day is never wasted. It is never too late in the day to start engaging with God. Keep the motor running, talk to the Lord all the time, and try to get disciplined about meeting with the Lord early in the morning.

Further Study: Luke 11:1-13, Ephesians 6:18, Romans 8:26

Shh! Get Quiet Before the Lord
Habits To Practice
Be still and know that I am God. Psalm 46:10

Sweet friend, God is for you and He eagerly desires to spend time with you. Please start engaging with the Lord. Are you lonely? If so, then please spend time with the Lord, because He is waiting for you to come to Him. But communication with the Lord is a two way street. Yes, one street is to tell Him everything, but dear friend, the other side of the street is that He also wants to speak to you. Shh! Be quiet in order to hear Him. Yes, you must get quiet and listen. Shh! Please do not be like the one who speaks for an hour, then only gives the friend one minute to speak. Please how about if we keep the conversation ten minutes of us talking and ten minutes of us listening to God speak? I hear you saying, "What? What? I have never heard God speak." Well maybe you haven't kept quiet long enough then. In order to hear, you must stop talking. You must start meditating on Scriptures, which is the primary way God speaks to us. Then I recommend you have a small journal or spiral notebook. As you pray and enter into the presence of the Lord, would you just jot down what you are sensing the Lord is telling you in the quiet place of your spirit? What is the Lord speaking? If you hear something jot it down. Then about two days later, come back and read what you jotted down. You may be very surprised to see that God spoke to you. So often we hear from God but we don't pay attention and recognize He has spoken. Other times we don't appreciate what we have heard.

Dear One, if you are a Christian, you have the creator of the universe speaking to you! That is magnificent and beyond comprehension. When He speaks you must listen and do all that He says to do. The more you practice listening prayer, jotting down what He is saying, and being careful to do all that He tells you, the better you will get at discerning His voice. Shh! Be quiet.

Further Study: Psalm 42:1, 1 Peter 3:4, Isaiah 30:15, Isaiah 32:17

Live Large! Receive Wisdom, Counsel, And All The Best Lectures!
Habits to Practice

> *If any of you lacks wisdom, you should ask God, who gives generously and it will be given to you. James 1:5*
>
> *Plans fail for lack of counsel, but with many advisers they succeed. Proverbs 15:22*

Okay, I can never say this often enough, God is for you and God's people are for you. Seeking counsel does not mean that you are going to be given orders to follow and you have to do what older ones dictate. No, it means that you are open to considering their input. Young people make an error and harm themselves, when they do not seek counsel. So my exhortation to you is this, "Please be open to wisdom. Do you want to be short on wisdom?" Sometimes we don't listen to wisdom because we are embarrassed by the gravity of our situation. Please take courage and go talk to someone. Yell at yourself if necessary and open your life to another believer whose life you admire. Open your heart to them, tell them your struggles, and ask them to help you see yourself more clearly.

What we've got to realize is that sometimes it is hard to get out of ourselves and see what we look like. You know how it is when you have a friend or relative you don't see that often and they are around twelve years old or so? Then you see that person six months later and my goodness, they've grown two inches and people make a big deal about their size change, but the child is like, well, no I hadn't even noticed I had grown at all. Truth is, when you are living with someone it is hard to see the change because they're living right next to it all the time. In the same way, it is hard to see yourself clearly because you are living with yourself, so you can be blindsided, you can have blind spots. God is saying to you dear friend, to be open first to hear from God what He has to say and second to hear from trusted Christians what they have to say.

I always joke with my students and say I need to give you lecture number 437 or lecture number 712. They laugh because I have so many things to say to them. But a wise teen, will welcome the lecture, the talk, the chat. The wise teen will give their mentor a chance to give them one of their lectures, because in doing so, they get larger faster!! Live large and always be open to growth in your life, willingly receiving input from others. We become stronger when we allow others to speak into our lives and advise us.

Further Study: Psalm 34, Proverbs 1:7, Proverbs 8, John 14:26, Romans 11:33, Colossians 1:9

Full of Self
Sins of the Heart

> *When pride comes, then comes disgrace, but with humility, comes wisdom.*
> *Proverbs 11:2*

When you are young it's all the rage to get the coolest guy or the hottest girl. And the higher up in the stratosphere of society you go, the more you begin to say, "Hey this is life and I've made it." Additionally there are other things that contribute to the pride of life including obtaining a powerful position, and plentiful possessions. The truth is that once you've reached the pinnacle of societal success one always knows that there is usually a downward spiral. The reason for the downward spiral is due to pride, arrogance, and losing sight of your need for God. There is a tendency to believe one's life and one's accomplishments have been obtained because of one's own self-sufficiency, beauty, and hard work. If we are not careful, we can puff ourselves up and forget that God sustains us. Dear friend, are you getting too full of yourself? Is it possible that you are forgetting God? Is it possible that you are about to take a downward tumble?

Do not be deceived dear friend, Scripture states pride comes before a fall. We like to wag our heads and stare through people and send off airs of superiority. We always like to look as though we have everything all together. We want people to believe we are one of the one hundred per centers, and that we are filled up. But the truth is that God views us differently. God is pleased with the person who recognizes that God is the one who gives talents to people and God is the one who sustains people's lives. Recognizing that all of life is a gift from God is what humility is. God says if we humble ourselves then we will be exalted. God is saying that humility is a choice. If it is a choice then it means we can choose to learn humility and we can practice humility. We need to understand that being authentic is good. To be real and to be in touch with the reality of having a variety of feelings and having a situation that is not always one hundred percent stable is normal. But if we are full of ourselves and are really convinced of how cool we are, we need to take a step back and meditate on our indebtedness to God. The truth is we are all in desperate need of God and anyone of us can forget this from one day to the next. Some of us are more willing to admit our need for God than others. When I am going into a situation and I sense that maybe I am arrogant, that's when I sit down and read through verses about humility. It is important to be filled with God, rather than be filled with self. We need to give thanks daily for the life God gives us.

Further Study: 2 Ch 7:14, Ezra 8:21, Ps 18:27, Ps 119, Prov 8:13, Is 66:2, Dan 10:12, Matt 11:29, Matt 23:12,Mark 7:14-23, 1 Cor 1:26, 1 Cor 4:18-19, 1 Tim 6:17, 1 John 2:16

The Light is Always On, You're Always Welcome to Come Back Home
Sins of the Heart

There will be more rejoicing in heaven over one sinner who repents than over ninety-nine righteous persons who don't need to repent. Luke 15:7 (Jesus)

The beautiful thing about Jesus is that He holds his arms open to you to come home even if you've been unfaithful. He always wants you to come back. Now that's not to say He won't be having a talk with you or won't want you to change your ways, yet still, He is always open armed. He beckons us, "Come on, come back to me." He deeply loves you. He deeply wants you.

It's funny, a friend told me the story of his life. He ran away from home when he was sixteen. He felt like he was the black sheep of the family, he felt he just didn't measure up. His brother seemed to be the strongest brother of the family. Well God got a hold of this man's heart and he returned to his family. The truth is that no one in any family should be labeled the black sheep with the connotation of not being as good as the other children.

I tell you this story to demonstrate to you that it is never, ever too late to come home. If you believe that it is too late for you, then you believe a lie. Satan comes to steal, kill, and destroy.

It is his scheme to make you believe you are not welcome back. I know God dear friend and I must tell you, He wants you back. His arms are open wide. Now your family might be a different thing. If you've offended them you might need to apologize, possibly they might never be the forgiving family you are hoping for. Regardless, God is the forgiving friend you have hoped for. God's heart is so big for you and filled with so much love for you, that He indeed welcomes you back. Psalm 23:4 says, "Thy rod and thy staff they comfort me." God's shepherding staff is His open arms which always welcome us back whereas the rod is the Lord's corrections that He sends our way. His corrections, his discipline are a comfort too. He will discipline you until you learn the necessary lessons that you have been trying to escape from learning. Discipline provides security and comfort because it lets you know what the rules are. Just like a horse track has fences around the perimeter of the track, God's discipline serves to let you know where safe boundaries exist for you to stay within, to protect you so you don't get hurt. Don't stay away from God, because you are afraid He will correct you, His corrections bring you life. Don't stay away from God because you are afraid He won't welcome you back. He is open armed! He loves you and He wants you to know, you are welcome to come back home to Him.

Further Study: Matt 18:11-17, Luke 15

Complacency-Who Cares Anyway? Let's Stay Warm and Comfortable
Sins of the Heart

> *You women who are so complacent, rise up and listen to me; you daughters who feel secure, hear what I have to say! Isaiah 32:9*
>
> *Because you are lukewarm-neither hot nor cold-I am about to spit you out of my mouth. Revelation 3:16*

Do you follow the tenets of Christ, agree with them, but have you become bored with living the Christian life? When we think to ourselves, who cares, I just want to be happy and comfy, what do we mean by that anyway? Listen, my kids know I have one pet peeve and that is food that is lukewarm. I like my hot food hot and my cold food to be cold. I like piping hot soup and a glass of frigid lemonade or ice cold milk. I find lukewarm soup unpalatable. Why? Like I tell my kids, if it's hot I know the bacteria are dead. Listen if you heat things to boiling, bacteria are killed. If food is left on the counter near the stove where it is warm but not hot, that is the danger zone where bacteria can multiply rapidly and you can have a food poisoning outbreak. Being uncaring or complacent for the things of God is like that. Being in the lukewarm zone is a place where you can have sin multiplying into an outbreak. It is like when acne suddenly multiplies into eruptions everywhere on your face. That is dreadful. A "sinfest" is also dreadful and is sure to result in casualties.

Wholesome living is a better way. Having a heart that is desiring after God is better than lukewarm living where sin multiplies and grows. Not passionately living for the Lord, but instead living with complacency, is living in the danger zone. No one lives exactly where you live, nor has the exact opportunities that you have to influence the world for Christ. You have great opportunities. If you have become complacent and uncaring, then look up! Follow after God and listen to Him for guidance on how to be involved in God's kingdom purposes. God loves it when you are on fire for Him. When you are on fire for God, it is then that you can live not with lukewarm comfort but in the realm of exciting possibility. Being on fire for the Lord, brings the joy of knowing that your life can impact the world for good. You can make a difference, your life and how you live matters.

Further Reading: Isaiah 32 Matthew 5,6,7

Reckless Behavior, You Are Worthy-You Are Someone Special
Sins of the Heart

> *Be careful to follow every command I am giving you, so that you may live and increase and may enter and possess the land the Lord promised you. Deut 8:1*

When I was young, reckless behavior was attractive to me. Even though I never indulged in reckless behavior, I still thought I was cool because I believed I didn't need to be careful. Yet as I've grown up I've become more careful and have shunned my attitude that carelessness is cool. More specifically, reckless living often has consequences that can be difficult to deal with.

A true story I heard is about four teenage boys. The parents of one of the boys, were out of town for the weekend, so all the boys went over to that home and started drinking. The boys had been instructed to never drink and drive, however, that night they made the critical decision to be reckless. However, before they did go out and drink and drive, around midnight, one of the four decided what was happening was not good. He chose to leave the situation and he went home. The other three boys continued to drink and then decided to go out at about two a.m. to get a burger. Recklessly they drank and drove that night resulting in one death, and one driver saddled with the guilt of having killed one of his friends. Now, you're thinking we've heard this all before, but I ask you, have you? God and caring parents do not give rules without reason. Parents say, be careful, so that you may live! God says be careful to obey my rules, so that you may live!

When you take care to be careful, what you are really saying is, I am valuable. I am worth being cared for. When you are reckless you are treating yourself as though you have no value! Furthermore, you are not listening to the heart of your parents or the heart of God who are telling you I want you to live and possess good things!! Believe that good awaits those who keep doing the things that preserve life rather than put themselves in the place where they might be destroyed. The truth is you are worthy, God and your parents think you are really valuable.

Now Scripture clearly denounces reckless behavior as described in the previous paragraph. However the word reckless is also used to describe four other things-destroying others so you can be put into power, using the Gospel to get rich, destructively lying about people, and falsely representing God to have said something that He hasn't said. If you struggle in any of these areas, you need to repent. Treat God and yourself like you truly matter and have nothing to do with recklessness.

Further Study: Numbers 22:32, Judges 9:4, Proverbs 12:18, Jeremiah 23:32, 1 Peter 4:4

Cultural Christianity-Jesus Is The Pizza Of Life
Sins of the Heart

> *You adulterous people, don't you know that friendship with the world means enmity against God? Therefore, anyone who chooses to be a friend of the world becomes an enemy of God. James 4:4*

Dear Ones, I mentioned to you earlier about Dave Phrase-putting the truths of God into interesting constructs in order to help us think contemporarily about Jesus' character. One of my all time favorite sayings that David created is Jesus is the Pizza of Life. One of David's friends liked this saying so much that he had it made into bumper stickers for David. Christian culture can be tricky. Culture has traditions, rituals, and forms to follow. If you follow the dictates of Christian culture you can be popular in your church and miss God! Potentially you could be two faced-a friend of Jesus and a friend of Christian cultural forms that miss God! You could love Jesus but not be allowing Jesus to shape the culture at your church into being a place where Jesus is welcome, a place where Jesus is the Pizza of Life, and a place that is first and foremost pleasing to the Lord. Are you clinging to your place in the Christian circle you find yourself in and clinging to practices and forms and traditions that keep the Lord out of your church? Friend, the truth is you cannot be a friend of the world and a friend of God, you must choose between the two.

We love and embrace community with Christians, however our primary alliance must be with Jesus! Our primary alliance in our churches needs to be on the side of God and allowing traditions and rituals and forms to change in order to allow the Spirit of God to flourish and be welcome even if it means giving up our position, our power, or our favorite program, if that is what the Spirit of God is telling us to do. More than anything we want the Lord's presence among us. The Lord is the one we welcome, He is our desire and the one who dictates our Christian practices. We meet together for the Lord! Worship is for the Lord! Church is the vehicle in which people can come and get to know the Lord. Church must be a place where Jesus can be known, experienced, and celebrated. When Jesus said, I am the Bread of Life, He meant that He must be the one you desire as much as you desire pizza!

Further Study: Matt 5:19, Mark 7:1-13, John 6:48, Col 2:8, Col 3:9, Rev 2:6, Rev 22:15

Special thanks to David Swarbrick, Jr. for creating the saying, "Jesus is the Pizza of Life".

Avoiding Greed-Who Is Your Taco Supreme?
Sins of the Heart

> *You cannot serve both God and money. Luke 16:13*
>
> *Be on your guard against all sorts of greed; life does not consist in an abundance of possessions. Luke 12:15*
>
> *But godliness with contentment is great gain. 1Timothy 6:6*

Dear friends, are you confused by this saying? What in the world did Jesus mean by this piercing statement that you can't serve God and money? Look closely at His word choice…you cannot what? You cannot serve money. Serve means to worship. Money worship occurs in the world. Jesus is not opposed to people making money, what He is opposed to is people placing supreme importance on money in their lives. God wants to be supreme. Is God your Taco Supreme or is Money your Taco Supreme? God is a jealous God and He wants to be the object of your worship, because you will miss out on Him if you do not worship Him Supremely. He wants to give you the rich gift of Himself. Okay, I get that you say, "But still why does He point out money?" He points out money because the pursuit of money can be so all consuming that it can begin to be the motivation for every decision that a person makes. Jesus calls us to choose to worship Him and to let pleasing Him be the motivation for the decisions we make. Money is necessary to conduct the business of life, but conduct that is becoming is rare. It's okay to utilize money, but it is not okay to let it consume all of our thoughts.

Now, no matter how much money people have, it seems like there is a tendency to never have enough and to always want more. Greed, the unending desire for more money and more things can enslave you to the point where even your physical life can become endangered. God is deeply for you and He is jealously for you to be free. Money worship can never bring you to the place of freedom and this is the reason why Jesus opposes it. On the other hand, contentment with what you have is good. Focus more on growing spiritually and becoming more like God. Growing in godliness is an excellent endeavor. I am so proud of you for pursuing godliness!

Finally, I am not giving you an excuse to be lazy and not work to develop your gifts. Work is important and a means to support you and eventually your family. So develop a skill to support you and your family and then be content with the lifestyle that skill supports. Most importantly, I want you to be free, free to work, free to be content with your financial place in life, free to make money to contribute to the Lord's work, and free to focus on the Lord, your Taco Supreme.

Further Study: Romans 12:13, Galatians 6:6, Ephesians 4:28

Avoiding Hypocrisy
Don't Be a Poser
Sins of the Heart

> *The teachers of the law and the Pharisees sit in Moses' seat. So you must obey them and do everything they tell you. But do not do what they do, for they do not practice what they preach. Matthew 23:2 (Jesus)*
>
> *Be on your guard against the yeast of the Pharisees, which is hypocrisy. Luke 12:1b (Jesus)*

For teenagers there seems to be a great temptation to be a poser. Somehow at this time of life we tend to feel a little vulnerable. We don't always feel comfortable letting people know what is going on inside of our hearts and so we plaster a smile on our face even though sometimes we are hurting. Being a poser means to wear a mask so that others believe something better about us than what is actually true. Some people get extremely good at this. This practice when it is repeated and refined as a behavior is in all actuality deceptive. A person who is a poser can get so good at faking things, they can get so good at getting others to believe things about them whether or not they are true. They can go so far as to fake that they're a Christian, but their actions tell a completely different story. It is as though they are always pretending. They are good at acting like a Christian but in reality they are not growing in the disciplines of being a Christian, they are not becoming a disciple. They are being a poser.

Now, I am not saying that people don't have struggles. Our actions can tell the story that we are struggling against sin, but our actions can also mean we are really enjoying practicing sin and we want to get better at sin. Which is it for you, struggling to get away from sin or actually enjoying your sin and reveling in it? Struggling to get away from sin is authentic Christianity. God is pleased with and looking for the development of your heart. People do have struggles. Struggling with a sin in order to move away from it is good. Israel means to struggle with God and to overcome. You do not have to tell people how you are doing all the time; you do not have to tell anyone and everyone what you are feeling or experiencing all the time. But it would be good, if you at least had one or two Christian friends who know deep down what you are facing. What I am saying is that I am so hoping that you will experience authentic Christianity and practice being authentic. Jesus' sharpest criticisms were for those who posed what their spirituality was and were content participating in evil deeds. Nothing was dealt with more severely. Don't be a poser, shun hypocrisy.

Further Study: Matthew 23, Mark 12:13-17, Luke 12:1-12, Galatians 2:11-21, 1Peter 2:1

Idolatry
I Like You, I Love You, Oops, I Worship You
Sins of the Heart

> *But Peter made him get up. "Stand up", he said, "I am only a man myself." Acts 10:26*
> *Do not worship any other god, for the Lord whose name is Jealous, is a jealous God. Do not make any idols. Exodus 34:14,17*

When we think of worship, we often think about worshiping other gods. Worship of other gods has been around for a long time. Back in the time of Christ, one of the many Greek gods was Artemis. One of the reasons the Greeks worshiped Artemis was because they were thanking her for giving them children. The truth is that God is the one who gives children. Today in our culture, instead of worshiping gods, we instead worship people like movie stars, sports stars, and we can even worship our Christian leaders. Sometimes we fall into the worship of men and women without realizing fully what we are doing. After Jesus ascended into heaven Peter was one of the leading Apostles, yet at one point people fell down to worship him. Now don't get me wrong, Peter was a great man of God, but he was wise and did not allow people to worship him, because Peter knew that worship belonged to God alone. We can honor people but we must not partake in people worship. Just like Peter the head of the early church was worshiped, people are still prone to worship famous people today.

Yes, people worship is idolatry. People worship occurs when you "over love" anyone. People cannot save you, you cannot save you, and you are not to worship people. For sure you should honor people but at some point one must realize the difference between honor and worship. Are the popular, pretty, happy, shiny people the ones whom you are trying to imitate? Is it the cool jock or the peppy cheerleader, or maybe even the counter culture guy because you admire his ability to be unique? So sure, all of these people may be interesting and they may even be Christian and some may even be worthy of honor, but you are only to worship God. God, only the triune God-God the Father, Jesus the Son, and God the Holy Spirit should be your waking prayer, the extreme object of your affection. Be careful if you idolize lest you engage in people worship. And most of all do not idolize yourself.

Listen dear friends, we need to understand the difference between worship and honor. It is acceptable to honor your parents, honor your teachers, honor your leaders, but it is not okay to worship any of them. God is a jealous God and He wants to be in the supreme place in front of all others. God is not okay with worship of other gods, worship of Peter, or worship of our boyfriend or girlfriend, our spouse or people in our lives. God alone is the one to worship. We worship God the Father, Jesus the Son, God the Spirit, the trinity, three in one.

Further Study: Acts 10, Exodus 8:1, Exodus 9:1, Exodus 23:25, 1 Chronicles 16:29, Luke 4:8,

Special Thanks to David Swarbrick, Jr and C.S. Lewis

Telling Lies, Flip Like A Burger
Sins of the Heart

> *The one who speaks the truth from his heart... who keeps his oath even when it hurts... He who does these things will never be shaken. Psalm 15:2,4,5*

We all know people who walk on both sides of the fence. We normally call them politicians. We laugh at this but the truth is that for some reason politicians can be caught saying different things to different people. During the election cycle we all listen and laugh when media types catch politicians flipping like a burger on certain issues for political expediency. And we all know that often the motive behind this is to get elected and to win the popular vote. Let me just say this, popularity is a fleeting value that can be here today and gone tomorrow. Instead of aiming for popularity, let's rather aim for integrity.

Integrity seems to be a lost family value. God values integrity and we need to stop lying to one another and start keeping our word. When we say things, they need to be true and when we give our word, we need to keep our word even if it hurts. The Psalmist lists speaking truth and keeping one's word as two of the hallmarks of a steady life that is built on solid ground. Dear ones, your integrity matters. Your character matters more than you know. Sometimes it is best to just be humiliated for the sake of practicing integrity. In our heart we think, well if they know I said I expected to be elected class president, then I will be humiliated if it is quoted what I said especially if I am wrong. The truth is that honesty can be uncomfortable. We must believe God's word that we will be better off in the long run if we tell the truth and accept any embarrassment, instead of lying and denying truth. The long-term gain of developing good character rather than the short-term reward of lessening our humiliation must be practiced. It is best to speak the truth from the start and then we won't have to go back and cover our tracks and admit we lied. But we all make mistakes and so we must learn to keep practicing telling the truth, and then eventually it will just become a part of our character, the inner man that reflects God who has integrity. So please stop changing your story, stop flipping like a burger, instead tell the truth and keep your word.

Further Study: Psalm 15, Proverbs 6:16-19, Proverbs 10:18, Proverbs 12:22, Zechariah 8:16, James 5:12

Sorcery, Divination, & Witchcraft
Sins of the Heart

> *Let no one be found among you who sacrifices their son or daughter in the fire, who practices divination or sorcery, interprets omens, engages in witchcraft. Deuteronomy 18:10*
>
> *The acts of the flesh are obvious: sexual immorality, impurity and debauchery; idolatry and witchcraft; hatred, discord, jealousy, fits of rage, selfish ambition, dissensions, factions and envy; drunkenness, orgies, and the like....I warn you... those who live like this will not inherit the kingdom of God. Galatians 5:19-21*

.

Dear Ones, it is important to realize that there is a spiritual battle that occurs daily. To engage in sorcery is to receive power or knowledge or help of any kind from evil spirits instead of from the Lord. People in the family of God should only accept gifts from the Spirit of God. The idea of sorcery and witchcraft is something the believer should have nothing to do with.

Simon is an example of someone who received power that wasn't from God. Acts 8 contains the record of Simon the sorcerer. Simon had a certain magical power that a great number of people found attractive. Simon appears to have repented and found the Lord. So we see that he repented, but we also see that he still had an ongoing battle with sin. Even though Simon was saved, Simon is seen trying to buy the power of God from the apostles. Peter rebukes him for this activity. Peter preached to Simon that Simon had to repent of the desire to purchase the power of God. The power of God is not something that can be bought.

In addition to sorcery being receiving from evil spirits, the Bible also shows that sorcery can be being inspired and led to do harm by evil spirits. The Bible provides several examples of witchcraft for us to learn from. In the Old Testament, Jezebel was one who killed God's prophets and she also engaged in witchcraft. Jezebel "crafted evil." One example of how she did this had to do with a man named Naboth who owned a vineyard. Jezebel wanted Naboth's property. In order to get it, she falsified documents in the king's name, set the kings' seal on the documents, and within the documents she falsely accused Naboth and had him stoned to death.

If the Lord has rescued you from occult practices, then it is important that you renounce anything you previously had to do with such activities and that you renounce any power you may have received that did not originate with God. Many times older Christians are able to help young ones who want to escape these activities by offering prayer for them.

Further Study: Deuteronomy 18:9-14, 1 Kings 18-21, 2 Kings 9, Acts 8:9-25, Acts 19:13-20, Revelations 2:20

Revenge and Jealousy-Hey Let Me Pay You Back
Sins of the Heart

Do not take revenge, my dear friends, but leave room for God's wrath, for it is written: "It is mine to avenge; I will repay: says the Lord. Romans 12:19

When you are a teenager it always feels like you are running out of money. So we often hear, "Can you loan me some money and I will pay you back?" Have you been there? If you are the one loaning the money you might wonder whether or not you are going to get paid back or not. Even crazier is when people become adults they are still running out of money and they are always living on debt or back pay. They are always outspending themselves and have not learned how to operate within their budget.

Sometimes when things happen to people in friendships, people let us down or we let our friends down. We hurt each other or we've been hurt by others. Maybe sometimes we will get to the good point of our friend telling us they're sorry or us saying we're sorry. We might even really mean it, but below the surface we know something is still really wrong and it's hard to put our finger on just what the problem is. And then the light bulb goes on and we realize that the person who we let down is into paybacks. They may have said they forgive us but deep down, they are living out of revenge and getting back at us. They are looking at us and saying, "Hey, let me pay you back." They haven't been able to let go of the hurt we caused them. Truth is, sometimes our heart does the same thing and we are tempted to say, "Hey let me pay you back."

Dear friends, these things ought not to be. Please stop the madness. If you are still mad at your friend and you are still hurt, do not lie against the truth. It's okay to still struggle with what happened in a friendship. What's not okay is to nurture resentment and revenge and to be into paybacks. Maybe you need a different friend, maybe you just need some time and space away from someone in order to get over what happened, or maybe you need to ask God to please take your anger away. Whatever it is, take your time, talk to a trusted mentor, pray and then make your decision to go forward without getting revenge, and without allowing your friends' paybacks to cripple you.

Further Study: Gen 4, Num 31, Deut 32:43, Rom 2:6, Rom 12:17-19, Heb 10:30, 1 Peter 3:9

Wholesome Living-Goodness, Gracious!
Growth In Christ

> *I have written both (my letters) to stimulate you to wholesome thinking. 2Peter 3:1*
> *Make every effort to add to your faith, goodness. 2Peter 1:5*
> *But the fruit of the Spirit is love, joy, peace, forbearance, kindness, goodness, faithfulness, gentleness, and self-control. Galatians 5:22-23a*

So here we are once again talking about wholesomeness and goodness. The Apostle Peter thought this was an important enough value to emphasize it with repetition and to state that this was the overarching reason for writing both of his letters. Wholesome living and goodness are important matters. We receive so many messages from the media that often we are confused about what we should value. Goodness gracious, God values goodness. If you happen upon a person in distress, help them out if you are able to.

I grew up in Wisconsin. A common problem in Wisconsin was the snowstorms. Oftentimes people would slide into a ditch with their car. You could see them rocking the car back and forth until they got the car out. Many times, a few people would stop to help, get behind the car and give the car a little bit of a muscle shove. That muscle shove would be enough to move the car from the ditch, to back on the road. It was a good deed that didn't receive an accolade. It was simply a kind thing to do. No one kept a record of what was done. No one received a standing ovation. No medals were awarded, and yet for the person who was helped it meant a great deal. God cares and He is blessed when you do good deeds *as unto Him.*

But it is not as though we should keep a record of the good we do, rather just make it one of your practices to do good deeds and then to just forget about it, moving on from strength to strength not keeping a record of what you've done, not publicizing it to anyone. Goodness, gracious, the goal is to please the Lord. The Lord knows our deeds; we live our life out to the Lord. We do good deeds as unto the Lord in thanks for all He has done for us. And as we bless the Lord with thank offerings of doing good deeds, our community is blessed and Christ is experienced whether we realize it or not. Be encouraged goodness matters and it strengthens the community around you in important ways. Be the change of goodness in your community.

Further Study: Psalm 84:7, Matthew 5:38-6:4, 6:19-24, 7:15-29; Ephesians 5:8-14, 1Timothy 2:1-7, 2 Peter 1:3, 2 Thessalonians 1:11

What Does God Want Me To Do?
Growth In Christ

> *To obey is better than sacrifice, and to heed is better than the fat of rams.*
> *1Samuel 15:22*
>
> *He replied, "Blessed rather are those who hear the word of God and obey it."*
> *Luke 11:28 (Jesus)*
>
> *I long to dwell in your tent forever and take refuge in the shelter of your wings.*
> *Psalm 61:4*

Don't let anyone despise you because of your youth. Because you are young, you can still be preparing yourself to do great things in the future, but you also can do great things for the kingdom of God now as a youth. The great things in your life can be huge if you choose to invest yourself in the kingdom of God. To be effective in investing yourself you mainly need to listen to Jesus. His words are the most important of all to listen to.

God really enjoys it when we live our life for Him, but God doesn't want us so much to sacrifice our time, He is really primarily interested in our spiritual formation. Spiritual formation means that we value having the right attitude and being the right person in the moments of our lives. He is interested most that we follow Him and obey Him. Sacrificial living is good, but obedience is best. You might ask, "Well how do I know what He wants me to do?" You know by studying and learning his Word and by listening to the voice of the Holy Spirit. He calls us to be a student of the Word. He also calls us to practice the art of listening to the Spirit of God. Once we hear from the Bible and from the Spirit what God is telling us to do, we can do it! The Scriptures say not to be just hearers of the Word, but doers of the word. We must do what the Word says to do. Then the joy comes! Then the healing comes! When we do what He says to do, He will reward us. If you are frustrated about certain sins in your life, don't focus on the sin. Concern yourself more with planting good things in the garden of your heart.

Plant God's Word in your heart, plant hearing His voice in your heart, plant singing worship songs in your heart. Before you know it, your heart will become a beautiful garden and sin will have lost its power there.

Jesus said, "The work of God is this: to believe in the one He has sent." Believing, doing the work of faith, living your life to please God is the most important spiritual work you can do. It is the great calling of the Christian life. If you are so consumed with serving and are burned out, then go back to the elementary teachings of seeking God and finding joy in your relationship with God, believing He will reward you for spending time with Him.

Now that you understand that the most important work that God calls you to do is your spiritual formation, you can then focus on learning to discern God's voice. Learning to discern God's voice takes time and practice. I do recommend that you obtain a spiral or a journal and a pen. Have these both at your bedside. When you are quiet before the Lord and saying your prayers, listen carefully. When you are quiet and hear from the Lord, write down what the Lord is speaking to you. For instance, if you are praying about what college you should attend. First tell the Lord you are willing to do what He knows is best for you. Second, write down the colleges you are considering. Then say Lord please speak to me about these colleges and what would be best for me. Quiet your soul before the Lord. Be still with the Lord. Then jot down any spiritual impressions you have from the Lord. Use these spiritual impressions to help guide your college choice. Seek the Lord in prayer. Listen. Jot down impressions. Obey whatever the Lord is telling you to do.

If you still are unsure about God's specific will for you, then you must walk forward in faith, following known principles. Do not violate what you know God values and make the best decision you can with the wisdom you have.

Further Study: Matthew 5,6,7; Hebrews 11:6, 1Timothy 4:1
Special Thanks to David Swarbrick, Jr.

Dealing With Temptation
Mastery of Subject or Mastered by Subject
Growth In Christ

And lead us not into temptation but deliver us from the evil one. Matthew 6:13

No temptation has overtaken you except what is common to mankind. And God is faithful; he will not let you be tempted beyond what you can bear. But when you are tempted, he will also provide a way out so that you can endure it. 1Cor 10:13

Dear Ones, when you are young, the world looks so bright and cheerful and a world of possibilities lie before you. So many good things present themselves to us. When you are young, it is almost as if the world is just a great big candy shop. There are so many things to try and experience and it all looks sweet. But many of us have been warned that some things that are promised to be sweet will actually result in bitterness. Hence, the goal for the young person is to become convinced of what to avoid. Now we know that rules do not constitute a lively Christian life and I am not suggesting to you that you follow a system of rules. For sure you are to follow Christ, and yet some things are just not profitable for you to partake in. This very question plagued the early church as they struggled to combine Jews and Gentiles into one group. As this new group of Christians was formed, they agreed on a common set of things to be avoided (Acts 15).

You will need to avoid certain things but you, under the tutelage of God the Father and your earthly parents, will determine what you can handle. Listen, being tempted to do the wrong thing is experienced by everyone, Christian and non-Christian alike. Now it is important to understand that God does not tempt anyone, rather that is the work of the evil one. God might test us, but remember the purpose of a test is to show your successful mastery of a subject not to make you fail. God wants you to master the subject whereas the evil one wants you to be mastered by the subject. When you are being tempted it is as though the evil one is whispering to you, eat this candy so I can rule over you and be in charge of you. God in contrast is saying if you master this candy and say no to it, then you will master it and you can take it or leave it whenever you want to. If something is a temptation to you, then it still has some power over you. The Lord wants you to be empowered over all things! The Lord wants you to be able to say no or yes to all things that are life giving and helpful to your days. The Lord desires to give you as much freedom as possible, however freedom is not being mastered by something, but freedom is the ability to be the master who freely chooses that which the Lord says is beneficial for you either in allowing it or disallowing it. Sometimes God says no now, but later on He says yes. Determine to not be mastered by anything.

Further Study: Matthew 6:5-15, Luke 4:1-13, Acts 10-15, 1Corinthians 6:12, James 1:13, James 4:17, 2Peter 2:19, IJohn 3:19-21

Pull A Paul Revere
Tell Someone What Jesus Has Done
Growth In Christ

> *Many of the Samaritans from that town believed in him because of the woman's testimony, "He told me everything I ever did." John 4:39*
>
> *Jesus said, "Go show yourself to the priest and offer the sacrifices that Moses commanded for your cleansing, as a testimony to them. Luke 5:12-16*

Most of us remember our history lessons, remembering when the word went out during the Revolutionary War that the, "Redcoats are coming, the Redcoats are coming." Paul Revere's famous ride provided people with warning; it gave them time to prepare. It was a call to arms of sorts. In the same way, when people give "their testimonies", it is a way of warning others and giving hope to others who are seeking truth, or seeking God. A testimony is a confirmation of a current reality. When many testimonies are heard, then more people take notice and try to figure out what is going on. People begin to be aware of the reality of God in the world.

A startling example of this was the history of the Samaritan woman. Jews and Samaritans were normally not close friends and this woman was so surprised Jesus was speaking to her because he was a Jew and she was a Samaritan. The startling encounter became even more interesting when Jesus had information that He was not normally expected to have-He let the woman know that she had already been through five husbands and was currently living with another man. As this woman experienced the power of God in Jesus' supernatural knowledge about her life, she was stunned into belief. She confirms Jesus' identity as a prophet and begins talking about her hope for the Messiah. As Jesus revealed to her that He was indeed the Messiah, then, wonderfully the woman pulled a Paul Revere-she goes and tells everyone. The beauty of this telling is that many people came to faith because of the Samaritan's woman testimony. Without it, they may have never known Jesus. So tell dear friend, do tell others what Jesus has done for you, because spreading the word, pulling a Paul Revere move, could save someone's life.

Further Study: John 4, Acts 1:8, Acts 3:1-16, Acts 5:17-42

Overcoming Shame-Chin Up, Take the Remedy
Growth In Christ

> *I confess my iniquity; I am troubled by my sin. Psalm 38:18*
>
> *Therefore confess your sins to each other and pray for each other so that you may be healed. James 5:16a*

Okay, so we all know that we have made some mistakes, but deep down there's a couple of things we don't want anyone to know about. I mean if they knew about that, well I would never be chosen to do anything. If you are in Christ you are chosen for great things, so how can this be? Well, that dirty little secret about what you did is eating away at your conscience. How could you have been so stupid? Well truth is, if it is eating away at you, then it probably wasn't good, but it doesn't have to keep you down. The good news is this: there is a remedy. When you are sick, your mom asks you to lift up your chin so she can pour into your mouth the cough syrup or the liquid antibiotic. You say, "Ugh, yuck", but you take it and in a few days you are feeling better. In the same way there is a remedy for the shame, but it is a little more painful than swallowing liquid antibiotics. Listen friend, do you want to get better? If so, then you need to do the hard work of telling the Lord and another person what you've done. Now I am not saying tell everyone, but I am saying do confess and tell at least one human being in addition to God, and get this sin off of your chest. Listen; there is value in confessing to God plus confessing to a human being. Confession to a human brings freedom from shame because there is the added element of accountability. Shame is like a mold that grows and multiplies in dark places. When light comes into the dark place, then shame's power is broken. Telling at least one person the truth of what you did breaks the power of shame and the hold that action has over your heart.

So, dear friend, "Chin up, take the remedy." Confess your sin to a counselor, a friend, someone who is trustworthy to pray with you and receive your confession without judgment. In this confession you will find freedom to move away from that activity, to renounce the deed done in darkness, and to never, ever do it again because you know it just won't be worth all the pain and turmoil that your soul experienced as a result.

Further Study: Leviticus 5:5, Leviticus 16:21, Numbers 5:7, Psalm 32:5, Psalm 51, 1 John 1:9

Get In a Group-Don't Survive, Thrive!
Growth In Christ

> *Jesus called his twelve disciples to him and gave them authority to drive out impure spirits and to heal every disease and sickness. Matthew 10:1*
>
> *After Jesus had finished instructing his twelve disciples, he went on from there to teach and preach in the towns of Galilee. Matthew 11:1*
>
> *After this the Lord appointed seventy-two others and sent them two by two ahead of him to every town and place where he was about to go. Luke 10:1*

Survival stories always intrigue me. We've all heard about the people who have survived at sea for a long time as well as people who have been lost in the mountains and were later found alive. It's always a thrill to hear when some of these lost ones are found and have survived. Why is it a thrill? It is a thrill because these stories are far more often tragic than victorious and so our hearts rejoice at the strength of the human spirit and the human will to live. Furthermore, it is tragic when we hear the story of a car crash or a plane crash and one is left and all other family members are lost. Many times lone survivors deal with what is known as survivor's guilt. Thoughts of, why did I alone survive, plague those who did not die.

People are not meant to live in isolation. When God created man, He said it was not good for him to be alone and hence the Lord God made woman. Intimacy, close human relationship is found in the family unit, but it is also found in the small discipleship group. What is experienced as fellowship in the larger body of Christ known commonly as the church is not the same as what is experienced in a small group. A small discipleship group is the example left to us by Jesus. Jesus met repeatedly with a small group. Jesus also did ministry together in the context of a smaller group. A close fellowship is achieved when smaller groups of people work together to advance God's kingdom.

This fellowship, this unity provides for intimacy, for closeness that allows factors that can come into play that do not normally work in the dynamics of a larger group. For instance, with a smaller group, honest questions can be voiced. Also debate can ensue which might strengthen one's ability to provide answers to people in the world who do not yet know Jesus. Debate in a small group can serve to strengthen. Additionally, confession of sin and remorse is more easily expressed with close friends, and prayer in a small group allows multiple people to be prayed for.

So yeah, sure survival stories intrigue us and are fascinating. But the question remains, which do you think is better, everyone thriving and living together or a lone survivor? The survival story might be thrilling, but living with close ones is life-giving. Teenagers and young adults who are wise will get in a group and learn how to live closely together with other Christians. It might not be a perfect group, but you will have a greater chance to not just survive, but thrive.

Further Study: Genesis 2:18, Leviticus 13, Psalm 25:16, Psalm 68:6, Ecclesiastes 4, Mark 1:45, Mark 4:10, Mark 9:2, Luke 5:16, Romans 14:7

Special Thanks to Matthew Swarbrick

Becoming A Shelter For Others
Growth In Christ

> *"But his delight is in the law of the Lord, and on his law he meditates day and night. He is like a tree planted by streams of water which yields its fruit in season"* Psalm 1
>
> *The salvation of the righteous comes from the Lord; he is the stronghold in time of trouble. Psalm 27:1*

The Christian life in some ways is a progression, you grow in grace and you develop Christ muscles. Over time you get stronger. So there are multiple works of grace over the course of a lifetime. Some works of grace like salvation are profound and foundational. Other works of grace are smaller and come about through placing bricks one at a time and before you know it, most bricks are in place. You become a strong building, a place of shelter that can accommodate many who are weak or who are struggling.

The Psalmist compared the person who meditates on God's word and who hangs out with God's people to a tree that is planted by a stream. Most of us have seen these large trees that are next to water sources. When a tree is planted by a reliable water source then certainly that tree will be a fruit-bearing tree. Similarly, when a Christian plants himself among God's people and asks for their advice he will be strengthened and grow in the ability to shelter others. Also, when a young Christian is in a group of Christians who are willing to not follow the crowd by being unkind and mocking the less popular kids, then more strengthening happens and one continues to grow in their ability to shelter others. Finally, when you as a Christian don't follow the crowd into being rebellious and going against the laws once again you are strengthened in your sheltering skills.

In Christ, you can become a shelter for others, a leader of others, and God might even choose you to become a watchman over others, but the requirement is that you must learn to watch over yourself first and master your appetites first. You must put to death the thought of being your own god, of mocking, and of rebelling against the rules. Once these thoughts are put to death and you practice making wise choices, then you will be fruitful and sheltering.

Further Study: 2 Samuel 22:1-4, Ps 9:9, Ps 18:2, Ps 37:39, Ps 43:2, Ps 52:7, Ps 144:2

I Don't Want to Grow Up
Peter Pan Syndrome
Personal Growth

Instead, speaking the truth in love, we will grow to become in every respect the mature body of him who is the head, that is, Christ. Ephesians 4:15

Consider him who endured such opposition from sinners, so that you will not grow weary and lose heart. Hebrews 12:3

Dear friend, it is difficult to be a teenager, there is so much that still has to be learned. The question is really; do you want to grow up? Growing up is painful literally and figuratively. Many kids, especially boys have growing pains because their bodies are growing so rapidly that it literally hurts. When your bones are rapidly growing, make sure you stretch before you go to bed at night. The growth of your ligaments has a hard time keeping up with your bone growth. Stretching exercises will decrease your pain. Likewise you've got to be stretched emotionally in order to be able to keep up with your physical and spiritual growth. Emotional growth is hard sometimes. Often we don't want to hear the truths because sometimes the truth is not spoken in kindness and our feelings get hurt. If we nurse our hurt and ignore the truth, then we will inevitably hurt ourselves in the long run. So, not to kill you, but to love you, please listen for the truth in what is being said even if it is not kindly spoken.

Listen, if you listen and take the truth and throw out the lies you will be stronger because of it. For example your friend might yell at you and say, "The problem with you is you are always borrowing my stuff and not returning it, I am sick of it." In your mind do you think, they are such a jerk for yelling at me and I am not going to listen to a word they say, or, do you think, they yelled at me and that is bad, but what they said is true so I am going to return all the things that I previously borrowed and was careless not to return? Listen, you can complain about the tone they used or you can choose to grow up, and filter the message for truth, even though the tone was unkind. You can choose to overlook how the message is delivered and grow from the truth or you can just feel bad and not learn from the experience and stay the same. Growth is a choice. Many of us know older people who are still acting like children; they have the Peter Pan syndrome…they don't really want to grow up. But you, you want to grow up. Please don't grow weary, don't lose heart, we are all learners, we all make mistakes, but if we are open to learning, then we will grow stronger faster.

Further Study: Proverbs 20:30, Proverbs 27:6, Luke 8:14, Ephesians 4:7-16, Colossians 4:12

Don't Accept Everyone's Opinion-Sneeze Well
Personal Growth

Who is the liar? It is whoever denies that Jesus is the Christ. 1John 2:22

Whoever claims to love God yet hates a brother or sister is a liar. 1John 4:20

Our friends around us tell us many things. As teenagers, you are bombarded with tons of messages. The problem is sometimes you don't know what to believe. Life seems so confusing at times. So herein is the problem, how do we filter through all of the information to keep what is true and to expel the rest? Well the most important thing is to know that you do need to expel certain things. You need not believe everything that is said. Listen, people speak lies every day. I once knew a woman who lied regularly. I heard her lie many times. I didn't respond to her, "Oh, you are such a liar." No, instead I made a mental note, she cannot be trusted and therefore I won't take what she says as true. I expel her testimony and instead look for truth from more reliable sources. I sneeze out false testimonies. I do not receive false testimonies about people. If I am hearing things about someone and it affects my relationship with them, then I will go to them personally and ask them what is happening. I give them a chance to speak about their life themselves and I let them know I am for them. False testimonies hurt people and is not for those who love God.

Other times when I need to sneeze well is on occasion when I have been told I am on the wrong track for following Jesus. When this happens, I will stand for Christ and I will defend

Jesus. I will not receive a slander against my Savior. I will vehemently sneeze that out. I will not let that slur enter my soul; I will not receive that lie. On still other occasions, there are lies that people will speak about me. If they tell me with their words or actions that they are against me then I will stand up for myself. I might or might not say something verbally, however certainly inwardly I will defend myself, and I will not receive their lie. I will sneeze the lies out. I will expel lies from my soul. Friends, you must learn to sneeze well. Vehemently sneeze out lies! Lies that threaten your Savior's Name, one of your friend's name, or that profoundly threaten your life situation or your identity in Christ cannot be received. Other less serious lies can simply be noted and that information can be tucked away in the recesses of your mind in case it is needed in the future. Be wise whom you are close friends with. Do not be close to a liar or someone who is filled with hate and hypocrisy toward you or toward Jesus. Do not receive lies, expel them and sneeze them out.

Further Study: John 13:34-35, John 14:15-24, John 15:1-17, John 21:15-17, 1Corinthians 13, 1John 3:10

Turtle Movements-Come Out of Your Shell
Personal Growth

> *And the peace of God, which transcends all understanding, will guard your hearts and your minds in Christ Jesus. Philippians 4:7*

I heard a story about a man who grew up in a war zone. Can you imagine being a kid and waking up to shelling and bombing every day? It took this man many years before he was able to recover from his bombed out childhood. The shelling got to him. Sadly some kids have grown up in homes that are verbal and physical war zones. Many of these teens walk around hurt, not fully understanding why they are wounded and not whole. Teenagers who have been hurt and have grown up in these types of homes, tend to develop shells-now I am not talking about macaroni shells, I am talking more like turtle shells. These types of homes result in the production of shells of protection. Protective shells temporarily preserve the inner man so that the mind and heart can somehow survive the devastation of destructive homes.

A turtle shell does afford protection, but it is not ideal. God has made humans to have their skeleton shell on the inside, so that their flesh is on the outside. This unique fleshy human face and body invites people into knowing your heart and your mind. If you are more like a turtle, then basically, you are shielding yourself from others and are less prone to allow others to get close to you. God has made us for intimacy, and without intimacy we get lonely.

So if you've grown a shell around your heart-stick your head out as you are able to. You don't have to come out all at once…just poke your head out and God will help you the rest of the way. Take initiative, call someone up and arrange to do an activity. Sometimes healing just takes time, but it definitely requires movement. Move out towards others in the strength and the faith that you have and God will give you more faith and more strength as you go along. Get up, get moving, even if your shell means you go slowly.

Further Study: Leviticus 25, Lev 27, Psalm 119:134, John 5:1-15, Galatians 4:5, Titus 2:14

We All Get Embarrassed
Personal Growth

> Nathanael said to him, "How do you know me?" Jesus answered him, "Before Philip called you, when you were under the fig tree, I saw you." John 1:48
>
> "I am the good shepherd; I know my sheep and my sheep know me." John 10:14
>
> "If you really know me, you will know my Father as well. From now on, you do know him and have seen him." John 14:7

So what is your most embarrassing moment? If you can tell it, it will take the sting out of it for you. The truth is everyone gets embarrassed sometimes. Life is embarrassing. For me, I can be disrespectful. I have embarrassed myself in the past by being disrespectful at times. Sometimes I have to move away from certain people if I am near someone around me who is saying bad things, less I fall into the trap of following them, because sometimes I can be led astray and follow the wrong speaker. My weakness is downright embarrassing. The way to avoid being embarrassed is not trying super hard to never be in an embarrassing situation. Freedom from embarrassment comes about when I deal with the underlying motives that are at the root of my wrong behavior or wrong attitude that is causing me embarrassment. God in His kindness has changed my heart, my heart now deep down desires to be respectful. Other common causes of embarrassment include things like an unrealistic desire for perfection or popularity. If we care too much what others think of us, we will be prone to embarrassment.

Dear Ones, most of my life I didn't care what people thought about me because I have always been a confident person, but through the years I've changed. Now I still don't care that much what others think about me, but what's changed is I care a great deal about what God thinks about me and my confidence is now in the Lord. By the grace of God I have moved away from being a disrespectful person into being a respectful person who profoundly honors others, because this is what God wants from me. I never want to disrespect people, because this displeases the Lord. Nowadays, I am more concerned with pleasing the Lord and not embarrassing my Savior. If I'm disrespectful I dishonor the Lord and that would cause me to be embarrassed. When I honor the Lord by treating others well, then I do not get embarrassed but instead am joyful that I glorified the Lord by having a kind attitude. Helping others by giving profound respect, speaking, "Yes, Sir" no matter what, exposes foolishness and alleviates embarrassment caused by sin.

Dear Ones, embarrassment is alleviated when we love the Lord above all else and have right motives. If there is something that truly embarrasses you, it can become your greatest strength as you practice the opposing behavior and become better at mastering your weakness. When you have mastered your weakness and replaced wrong motives with the motive of pleasing the Lord in all you do, then you will be confident in the Lord, and embarrassment should dissipate.

Further Study: Psalm 139:1, Mark 6:32-34, John 4:1-26, John 14:5-14

Waiting Tables
Would You Like A Cup of Guilt With That?
Personal Growth

> *Let no debt remain outstanding, except the continuing debt to love one another, for whoever loves has fulfilled the law. Romans 13:8*

> *But King David replied to Aranuah, "No, I insist on paying you for it. I will not sacrifice to the Lord my God burnt offerings that cost me nothing." 2Sam 24:24*

Discerning what others are saying to us takes practice. It is not always easy to clearly delineate what people really mean. People don't normally make it so clear as to ask if you would like a cup of guilt with your dinner. Guilt would be a funny thing, except for the fact that it's destructive.

A clue that someone is using guilt to coerce you into a certain activity is words like "you owe me" or "remember when I did such and such for you…" So yes, these are not loving words because they imply that the one speaking is holding something over you, he is trying to hold you captive to his desired action he has planned for you and if you don't do it, there's a sense that you're not doing what is required. Sometimes people "guilt you" into performing for them out of a perceived debt that you owe them. Now you are thinking, how can this be? I didn't take anything from them, did I? The answer is yes, you might have. Think carefully and ask yourself if you asked this person for help with homework, a ride home, part of his lunch, or a myriad number of other things. If you did receive something and this person guilts you, then your friend did not have the ability to give to you freely.

Listen, these things ought not to be, but the reality is that people struggle even though they are Christians. God desires that we do things out of the motive of love not out of the motive of guilt. In truth, you can only be guilted into behavior if you allow it. Number one, if you know someone has a tendency to "guilt you", then you should try to avoid being in debt in any way to that person-financially or emotionally. You should not accept gifts from that person; instead you should maybe trade an orange for an apple or pay them for any goods or services you receive. The Scripture says not to be in debt to anyone. Paying for things prevents being "indebted" to other people and being "guilted" into their prescribed behavior they are demanding from you. It is best practice to avoid receiving large gifts from people (other than family) without paying for it-especially if that person does not seem to be able to freely give to you.

You can also ask the Lord for help if you yourself have a tendency to guilt others. If this is your struggle, then you need to practice giving freely without expectation of repayment. God loves it when you give, but for you, it might be better not to give until you can give freely with your heart, without expectation of being paid back. If you want to be paid back, then be clear and up front in your communication that you need to be paid back and within a certain timeframe. Don't blame others for what you have not openly and clearly communicated.

Further Study: Matthew 10:1-10, Mark 10:21, Mark 12:1-17, Luke 6:27-36, Luke 11:5-13, Acts 5:1-11, 1Corinthians 2:6-16, 2Corinthians 9:7

Dealing With Discouragement-"Defeatgate"
Personal Growth

> *If anyone gives a cup of water to one of these little ones who is my disciple, truly I tell you, that person will certainly not lose their reward. Matthew 10:42 (Jesus)*
>
> *You know that the Lord will reward each one for whatever good they do, whether they are slave or free. Ephesians 6:8*

Back during the Nixon Presidency, there was a scandal called Watergate. Watergate occurred when the Republicans broke into the Democratic headquarters in order to obtain information. Watergate was a scandal of sorts that defeated President Nixon and eventually he was impeached. As Christians we might at some point lose a place or a job and we feel we have our own scandalous "Defeatgate". We get discouraged because our life is not all that exciting and we are plodding along doing the work of the Lord and we suffer a setback of some sort and also we are not getting any acclaim for what we do. And there are others alongside of us and it seems as though they are both having success and getting attention. We are living our life to the Lord, not to other people. The Lord must be our focus and as we humble ourselves He will lift us up if we need to be lifted up. The Lord will rescue us from "Defeatgate".

When I have been discouraged, I have found that one of the best encouragements was to look upon others who were in a worse situation. It is helpful to take your eyes off of yourself and fix your eyes on those who are suffering. There is nothing so humbling as visiting a cancer ward, or a third world country where resources are few and far between. We can of course, also fix our eyes on Jesus who suffered so greatly. In remembering Jesus' betrayal, the torture He endured, His imprisonment, and His crucifixion, it is very difficult for us to really pity ourselves. What we must remember is to focus on the correct things. We must sharpen our focus; we must correct the setting of our lens so to speak. As we look on life with God's perspective of focusing on Jesus, we know we are not alone in our struggle and we take heart because we have an example to follow.

One of the things that people long to hear is, I am proud of you. So if you need to hear this today, I am going to say it, "I am proud of you for following Jesus as a young person. I am proud of you. If you are following Jesus, it is a brave thing to do." We all know how tough it can be to be a teenager, but to stand for Jesus as a young person is an awesome thing to do and it takes courage, so keep doing it. Keep plodding along doing your little thing because your little thing is something that matters to the Lord and it helps to change the world.

Further Study: Job, John 16:33, 1 John 5:4

Please Hurry Up and Make Me Patient

Personal Growth

But the fruit of the Spirit is patience. Galatians 5:22

Through patience a ruler can be persuaded, and a gentle tongue can break a bone. Proverbs 25:15

A man's wisdom gives him patience; it is to his glory to overlook an offense. Proverbs 19:11

When I was a teenager I really started getting into God. I mean God broke through into my life in a powerful way. I felt God's presence and I desired to have more of Him in my life daily. He was a bright spot. I tend to get enthusiastic about things and I was enthusiastic about God. Coming from a family of nine, the acquisition of food was a full time job. Planting in the garden, applying fertilizer, watering, weeding, then finally picking, washing, and freezing or canning, or just cooking for dinner. Well, one day I was so excited about God and on a spiritual high and I was praying for more patience, which I had noticed, was a spiritual weakness of mine. I mean I was begging for patience. Do you understand, I was basically demanding it from God? Give it to me now or else I am going to die sort of thing. So God dutifully answered my prayer. My mom asked me to put a bunch of food in the freezer downstairs. I took all the food down and started shoving it into the upright freezer. When you have a big family, a freezer is your best friend, however as soon as I shoved one bag in, another item fell out. This seemed to go on forever until I cried out in exasperation, "God you don't have to teach me patience all at once do you?" God is kind of funny that way. We had a good chuckle about that together. The funny thing was as soon as we had our laugh, I easily got everything neatly placed in the freezer and firmly shut the door.

Patience is something you acquire over time. Works of grace take time. The cool thing is spending time with Jesus reaps rewards. If you hang out with Him, you become like Him. So patience isn't something you acquire by effort, rather it comes because of your lifestyle of prioritizing spending time lifting your spirit up to the Lord with adoration in private and corporately, and lifting your needs up in prayer in private and corporately.

If you struggle in the area of patience, you probably need to look at patience differently. Patience is an arrow to add to your character quiver. If you learn patience by hanging out with Jesus, then you will be strengthened in the inner man. If you have patience as part of your character you can even persuade those who are powerful over you. Solomon declared that the strength of this character trait means you can break things that need to be broken (Proverbs 25:15). Sometimes bad habits take concerted effort to get rid of. Some unwise traditions need to be broken free from. Some leaders need to be convinced. Some followers need to follow. Jesus can help us individually or corporately in our communities to break free from anything that is having power over us. However, that help comes more swiftly if we are able to deal gently and patiently with those we are trying to influence.

Another goal is to become more patient with other people and to be patient when they do things wrong. Solomon declares it is a glory to overlook other people's shortcomings (Proverbs 19:11). What does this mean? It means your character becomes so strong that you can recognize others fail and leave room in your heart for failings. People of weak character throw fits when others get it wrong. People who are strong understand that people are growing in the Lord at different rates and the strong don't need to expose every time others fail. Overlooking an offense shows how strong you are in the Lord. Now I am not saying to overlook major things, but I am saying to be able to quickly forgive the little things like someone having a shorter temper than usual because they are stressed out, or someone forgetting an appointment with you. These types of annoyances should be able to be quickly overlooked as long as they are not repeated, ongoing patterns of behavior.

Further Study: Proverbs 14:29, 15:18, 26:32, Romans 12:12, ICorinthians 13:4, Ephesians 4:2, Colossians 3:12, 1Thessalonians 5:14, James 5:7-10

Enlarging Boundaries For Others

Celebrating Freedom

> *It is for freedom that Christ has set us free. Stand firm, then, and do not let yourselves be burdened again by a yoke of slavery. Galatians 5:1*

> *The Lord is the Spirit, and where the Spirit of the Lord is, there is freedom. 2Corinthians 3:17*

Sometimes we get frustrated when people don't act the way we think they should. In our mind we say, "Well if they really loved God then they would be with me all the time, they would make me their first priority when they see me at church or school, etc." Most of these expectations often have to do with our personal disappointment that we aren't more important to people. We don't give them freedom because we feel hurt. We attempt to control others and keep them boxed in to our expectations in order to minimize our hurt. Dealing with personal rejection by forcing people into a box is not wise and it is not of the Lord. God gives freedom. Freedom means the ability to move without restraint. God loves adventure and movement and exploration. And God wants our life with Him to be adventurous. Now I am not supporting a freedom where we indulge in sin, no I am saying a holy relational freedom to live an adventure-filled, Jesus-life.

So the problem really is, what do I do with my hurt if I find myself with a lot of expectations for others to treat me in prescribed ways? Well, of course the answer is to bring it to the Lord in prayer. Once you trust the Lord with your hurt, you can find peace with giving people their space and not demanding and expecting a certain boxed behavior that you dictate for others, but instead, freely enjoying and accepting with a thankful heart when you do receive attention from people rather than demanding attention. We should make wide spaces for people to live in so that they experience the freedom of the Lord. If we make wide spaces for them, then we are more able to have a healthy, undemanding, fruitful relationship with them. Giving people freedom means we become more comfortable with a greater expanse for them to operate within. In enlarging boundaries we give people their freedom, but we also are then able to enjoy people more freely which oftentimes will mean people are more open to give us attention because we are simply more enjoyable to be around.

Further Study: Ezekiel 19, Acts 21:37-28:31, Genesis 37-50, Matt 5:25, Matt 14:3, Matt 18:21-35, Acts 8:3, Acts 12, Acts 26:10, Rom 16:7, Hebrews 13:3, Revelation 2:10

Freedom Does Not Mean License-"Level Up"
Celebrating Freedom

> *There are ungodly people, who pervert the grace of our God, into a license for immorality and deny Jesus Christ our only Sovereign and Lord. Jude 1:4b*

So my youngest son William got his license a few years ago. It's always fun to get your license because it means having a greater sense of freedom and responsibility. When Will got his license it meant he could drive himself to school and drive himself to his basketball practices. It took sixteen years to get to that point. Sixteen years is a long time. Will practiced driving since the day he was fifteen because that is the day he got his learner's permit. He practiced a lot. But even more than that, he had fifteen years of riding while other people drove. Will learned from watching other people drive, he learned from others. He had fifteen long years of watching his mom and dad drive. Now, he wasn't always thinking about learning driving skills while he was riding along while one of his parents drove the car, but he still learned.

So, first of all, license means you have been paying attention for a long time and you have been practicing a long time. License also means you gain freedom to level up into having greater responsibility-not freedom to do bad things. As you hit the road on your own, your license *makes you the one responsible* to keep aware, to not text and drive, to be polite, to not speed over the posted limit, to stop at stop signs, to use your blinker and to never ever drink and drive or get into a car with someone who has been drinking or drugging. Getting a driver's license means, yes you can go places on your own, but you are now the one who makes driving decisions where in the past it was your parents. Being given a license means you can be trusted to level up into the responsibilities that come with freedom. Being given a license means you better not be foolish or the license might be taken away and you might no longer have the freedom to drive.

Well similarly, as you have increased freedom when you obtain a driver's license, you likewise have increased freedom in the Lord as you walk with Him. This freedom doesn't mean that all of a sudden you have a license to do bad things, things that you know would be detrimental to your soul. Rather, having freedom in the Lord means you have gotten to a point spiritually where you have walked with the Lord and been a disciple for quite a long time and you have broken free from at least some of the spiritual bondages that beset you and you don't want your license-your freedom-in order to go around and do harmful things. You are not a fool. You realize that walking with the Lord means you are boldly living for Jesus and you are not going to be greedy and steal from God's people, you are not going to be sexually immoral, nor will you use force against those who are younger in Christ. You have learned how to master your spirit, and thus you are not concerned with rule following to the point where you are constantly thinking legalistically. You know that doing negative things or just being a rule follower is not really fruitful. So it is kind of like you've learned to "level up". You can be trusted with more responsibility in the Lord, because you have developed your muscles in Christ, you have strengths in Him, so you can "level up." You are going to "level up" and love the Lord and not "level down" and be a libertine or legalist. Your freedom is a license to "level up" to serve the Lord, not a license to "level down" to do evil by being greedy, being immoral or by using force against your brothers or sisters in Christ demanding they serve you.

Further Study: 1 Samuel 2:12-4:22, 1 Samuel 1-2:11, 1 Samuel 7

God Enlarges Boundaries For Us When We Are Ready For That Freedom
Celebrating Freedom

Submit yourselves for the Lord's sake to every authority instituted among men: whether to the king, as the supreme authority or to governors, who are sent by him to punish those who do wrong and to commend those who do right. For it is God's will that by doing good you should silence the ignorant talk of foolish men. Live as free men, but do not use your freedom as a cover-up for evil; live as servants of God. 1Peter 2:13-16

There is neither Jew nor Gentile, neither slave nor free, nor male and female, for you are all one in Christ Jesus. Galatians 3:28

Dear Ones, so one of the greatest challenges for young people is to subject themselves to authority. Within every community there are rule givers, rule followers, and rule breakers. The Scriptures teach plainly that God has instituted authorities and we are to follow the rules. Being a good follower is a prerequisite to being a good leader. If you cannot follow well, then you will have a problem leading. So steel yourself to go along with leadership and to subject yourself to authority. Listen everyone has to subject himself to leadership. Before David killed Goliath, he went and spoke with King Saul and *asked permission* to fight Goliath. Before Moses left Egypt he went to Pharaoh and asked Pharaoh to let the Israelites leave. The examples are endless. The centurion rightly testified that when he gave orders to the soldiers under him, they did as they were told. If you can't follow a leader then you are going to struggle. All who want to lead must follow, and all who follow well, are potential leaders of the future.

The apostle Peter most certainly sees the benefit of being blameless and following leadership as a means to silence ignorant men. What is the benefit here? It becomes very difficult to not look foolish when you attack someone who has carefully done all that they are supposed to do, serving the Lord from the heart and not hiding wrong doing. It is easy for people to see through someone who attacks a blameless one. Consider this, if you've fixed your bed, hung up all your clothes, and vacuumed your room and someone comes in and says, "Look at this pigsty, clean up your room," what will be the response? The person criticizing your room looks pretty ridiculous and everyone can see that they are the one missing the mark. Basically that's what Peter is saying. Peter is saying be excellent so that foolish people just really can't find any dirt on you. But he also says there's freedom. Sure you're disciplined and sure you follow the rules and practice excellence, but you also know you are not in bondage. If you don't really like someone's leadership style you can work for a different company or you can attend a different church. You aren't forced to stay in a bad situation, but neither should we be changing jobs or our church every year! You can freely make choices within God's system of values, choices like who to marry, where to go to college, what neighborhood to live in and what career you will do. God allows breathing room. God doesn't suffocate us. He gives us larger boundaries when we are zealous for Him and when we subject ourselves to authority. We can be given authority when we can subject ourselves to authority.

Jesus also says there are some special considerations. One, *if the ruler's not good and you cannot escape the authority situation you are in, then you must submit to their rules anyway, but don't be like the ones who set rules but don't practice what they preach.* The other special case is when men set themselves up over God. In this case, God must be followed supremely over following the rules of men.

Further Study: Esther 9:29, Proverbs 29:2, Matthew 7:29, Matt 8:9, Matt 20:25, Matt 21:23-27, Luke 19.17, Hebrews 13, James 1:4, 2 Peter 2:13-25

Having a Clear Conscience-Don't Be Shipwrecked

Celebrating Freedom

So I strive always to keep my conscience clear before God and man. Acts 24:16

Search me, God, and know my heart; test me and know my anxious thoughts. See if there is any offensive way in me, and lead me in the way everlasting. Psalm 139:23-24

Holding on to faith and a good conscience, which some have rejected and so have suffered shipwreck with regard to the faith. 1Timothy 1:19

Having a clear conscience is a blessing when you have it. If your conscience is muddied it will dog you. If you are dirtied, you've got to get a shower and get cleaned up. Sometimes we have little habits that we don't even realize are negative and they are muddying our souls. Other things are more severe and one time sins where we give in to an impulsive lust of the flesh. Other things are bad practices that are engrained into the fabric of who we are that need surgical removal and need to be replaced with a Jesus habit-a habit where we become more focused on Him and doing His work in the world.

So now that we accept that we can get dirty, one of the habits of a spiritually maturing disciple is to get washed up. The imagery of washing is all over Scripture. The Pharisees got the ceremonial part of washing down, but they missed the heart of washing. Washing is a picture of living according to conscience. Every time the Pharisees were washing they should have had a heart that was willing to be purified and cleaned up on the inside. The interior life of determining to enter into the process of sanctification is to live by conscience. Young Christians do not always know certain things are wrong, but as you grow up, you learn what is wrong over time. As you learn things are wrong, then you must move away from partaking in those wrong activities or impure thoughts or bad attitudes. The important thing is not to let one bad choice be repeated over and over again, ignoring your conscience and ending up with a deeply engrained sinful habit in your life. If you keep on practicing things that you in your heart are convinced are wrong for you, then you are choosing to ignore your conscience and are in danger of being shipwrecked. If on the other hand, you learn something is wrong and then you stop doing it, you will enjoy the benefit of a clean conscience and enjoy clear sailing.

Strive to live by your conscience. If your conscience is telling you to stop, if there's a check in your spirit, then do not do the thing that the check in your spirit is warning you against. The check in your spirit is like the engine light in your car that warns you that something is wrong. If you follow your conscience and the checks in your spirit, then you will not shipwreck your faith. Quickly respond to the Lord when your check engine light goes on, don't reject the warnings. There is much peace in living out one's life before the Lord and having a clear conscience. Your conscience is a gift. Living to have a clear conscience is what in the end produces a free heart. To have a free heart is like sailing on calm waters, it allows you to move forward into the work of the Lord with joy and without worry of being shipwrecked.

For Further Study: Hebrews 13:18, 1Peter 3:16, 2Corinthians 1:12, 2Corinthians 4:2

Living the Abundant Life
Celebrating Freedom

> *I have come that they may have life and have it to the full. John 10:10 (Jesus)*
> *Take delight in the Lord, and he will give you the desires of your heart. Psalm 37:4*

God is for an abundant filled, purposeful life for all of us in Christ. In order to have abundance, we must continue to grow in our faith and delighting in the ways of God. As we delight in the Lord, then our desires become His desires and we become caught up in the Lord's mission on earth. Jesus did come to show us the way to heaven, but Jesus also died to give us heaven here. When Jesus said I came to bring you life and life abundantly He means He can and does give meaning and purpose to our days now. The thing of it is if you want life you must want Jesus because He is the source of life. If you keep trying to get life outside of Jesus you will be disappointed and you will miss abundant life.

When Jesus was teaching on the abundant life, He said that He is not like a hired hand, who runs away when the wolf comes. No, instead Jesus said he is the Good Shepherd who will lay his life down and take on the wolf, He will not abandon his sheep and allow them to face the wolf alone. Jesus laid down his life for the sheep, He does not abandon his sheep. We are the sheep and Jesus is the Good Shepherd. Because of Jesus' coming we have someone to follow, someone who showed us how to live. The shepherd left the goodness of heaven to bring goodness to earth. Now we can do likewise. We can lose ourselves in the purposes of God and bring goodness to the world. Jesus has shown us how to do it, we can become like Him.

It is in this way then, that we begin to experience the abundance that starts on the inside. By dying to self and living for God, we become life-giving people. We become big hearted, we ourselves begin to be a resource for others instead of a drain on others. We begin to richly enjoy all things instead of trying to get richer in order to have all things. Jesus teaches us, His disciples, how to give and how to hold things loosely. Jesus teaches us how to live richly toward others, living unselfishly to enrich others.

Now I am not saying I believe in a prosperity Gospel. Hebrews 11 mentions those such as Moses and Rahab whose lives were spared because of their faith, and others who suffered because of their faith and were jeered, flogged, chained, and even put to death. Yet they *all* were commended for their faith. Jesus did not promise an easy life, He promised abundant life, life that continues to well up in one's soul for those that are delighting in Him. Those who delight in the Lord, will find abundance to live a life of purpose, doing the good that the Lord prepared in advance for them.

Further Study: Psalm 1, Matt 6:19-21, Matt 19:23-24, Luke 3:14, Luke 6:38, Luke 12:13-33, Luke 18:22, John 10:1-21, 2Corinthians 4:7, Ephesians 2:10, Philippians 4:11-12, 1Timothy 6:8, 1Tim 6:19, Hebrews 11, Hebrews 13:5

Special Thanks to Pastor Mike Kaylani

In Transition: Kingdom Advancement, Things Changed After Jesus Died and Was Resurrected

Understanding the Holy Spirit

> *"There was a man sent from God whose name was John…he came as a witness….he confessed freely, I am not the Messiah….the one who sent me to baptize with water told me, The man on whom you see the Spirit come down and remain is the one who will baptize with the Holy Spirit." John 1:19-28*

> *He must increase, I must decrease. John 3:30 (KJV)*

> *But very truly I tell you, it is for your good that I am going away. Unless I go away, the Advocate will not come to you; but if I go, I will send him to you. John 16:7*

When you enter God's house, and become a child of God, you enter God's kingdom and pass from death to life. And as one who has entered into life, you should understand who people are. First of all, there was a man named John the Baptist. Now, John had a clearly defined mission, he prepared the way for Jesus to come. In John 1, the Baptist makes it clear that he is not the Messiah. John's role was to spiritually prepare folks for Jesus' coming. We might call him Mr. Assist. He told everyone the spiritual work they needed to do to get ready for the Messiah. He told everyone to repent. This is how the Baptist assisted Jesus. If you play sports you understand the concept of making an assist. Assists are counted in team stats because they powerfully help a team win. John the Baptist was not the star, instead he was "Mr. Assist" who helped us win, he prepared the way for the star, Jesus, to come and be dominant.

If you play sports, you also understand that many times games are won or lost in transition. In sports, transition defense means how good your defense is at the beginning of the time when your team no longer possesses the ball. Transition offense means how good your offense is at the beginning of the time when your team first gets the ball. Similarly, it was a time of transition when John the Baptist prepared for Jesus to come; when Jesus did come; and then when Jesus left and the Holy Spirit came.

As Jesus became more and more prominent, John understood he had to get out of the way. John was imprisoned and eventually beheaded. John's job, the assignment John had received from God was done, his assistance and the transition were completed.

Once John was gone and Jesus was leading, Jesus made it seem like His leaving to go to heaven was a good thing. But how could the Holy Spirit, someone who couldn't be seen physically, be better than someone who was currently present bodily? The way to think about that is as follows: Jesus was bodily one person and so many people wanted to be with Him, and only one man for say a million people, well you can see it would be hard to keep having conversations with all those people bodily. It is as though Jesus was saying, "Hey, it's good I'm leaving because then everyone who wants to, can be talking to me at the same time." Jesus suffered, died, and was resurrected. In Acts we learn the Holy Spirit came to all believers. Nothing would ever be how it used to be. Things were changed forever. Transition went smoothly and effectively just as planned. The Baptist had paved the way for Jesus, and Jesus had paved the way for the Holy Spirit. Jesus' life, death, and resurrection, was God's provision to atone for sin to reconcile men to God. Satan thought he would win by killing Jesus, but instead he lost. Because now, we are in the thick of our offense, not at the beginning of it. The Holy Spirit is in the house!! The Holy Spirit has been operating in the house of believers for over two thousand years now. The Holy Spirit living inside of us fills us with spiritual joy. The good news is that the Spirit is not only reserved for a few, it is not only for the Jews, and it is not only for free men. Rather the Spirit has been poured into all believers, Jew or Greek, male and female, slave or free. Anyone who is saved has the Holy Spirit living within Him.

Further Study: Mark 6:14-29, John 1:29-34, John 3:22-36

Trinity-One God, Three Persons
Understanding the Holy Spirit

> *Jesus was baptized too. And as he was praying, heaven was opened and the Holy Spirit descended on him in bodily form like a dove. And a voice came from heaven: "You are my Son, whom I love; with you I am well pleased." Luke 3:21b-22 (Jesus)*
>
> *...God chose you as first fruits to be saved through the sanctifying work of the Spirit and through belief in the truth. He called you to this through our Gospel that you might share in the glory of our Lord Jesus Christ. 2Thessalonians 2:13-14*

Well so yes, God lives in your house, but now you also live in a new kingdom. As you enter into this new kingdom it is important to be introduced to everyone, to say hello and to understand who lives in the kingdom where you now live. If you are in Christ, then you are now living in a new kingdom. You need to understand how the kingdom is governed. The kingdom is governed by the trinity and so you must understand whom the trinity is. God is three persons in one is what the word trinity means. God is the Father, Jesus is the Son who provides atonement for our sins, and the Spirit is the one who lives inside of us.

When Jesus was baptized, we have the historical record to the presence of all three parts of the trinity. The witnesses to this event recorded hearing the audible voice of God the Father, of seeing the physical Jesus the Son being baptized, and of seeing the Holy Spirit descend on Jesus in bodily form *like* a dove. Now, this in itself was a miraculous event. Jesus the Lamb of God was baptized. The audible voice of God was heard. The manifest presence of the Spirit was seen.

The manifest presence of the Spirit can be experienced by the believer, but this manifest presence was truly miraculous and noteworthy. The Spirit was manifested in a way that could be physically experienced by those present, *similar* to the way a dove could descend onto a person. This was a glorious event in church history.

The Spirit is the third person of the trinity. The Spirit is the one whom dwells in us. The three in one is a great mystery. God is one, but is three distinct persons. Although you can't see the Spirit of God, He is real and you can sense His presence. The Spirit is God just as much as God the Father is God and Jesus the Son is God. It is a great mystery this three persons, who are all one yet are all distinct. As a person who now lives in God's kingdom, you will encounter all three persons of the trinity as you follow the Lord. You will understand the mystery more deeply as you go along.

Further Study: Deuteronomy 6.4, Mark 12:29, John 1:32, 14:16-18, 15:26; Colossians 1:13

Special Thanks to Rob Harrell

It's The Real Deal, We're Sealed

Understanding the Holy Spirit

And you also were included in Christ when you heard the message of truth, the Gospel of your salvation. When you believed, you were marked in him with a seal, the promised Holy Spirit, who is a deposit guaranteeing our inheritance. Ephesians 1:13-14a
And do not grieve the Holy Spirit, with whom you were sealed for the day of redemption. Ephesians 4:30

When I was a new Christian, I didn't know very much about following Jesus. I went to Bible studies, prayer meetings, and many different churches. Everything was new and fascinating to me. I was born again and I was learning there were a variety of Christians. Some practiced things one way and some another way. They were all Christian but they just varied in their practices.

As I grew in the Lord, I became more aware that some Christians were uncertain of things. In the Bible we see the process of people not being certain about things when Jesus was crucified, died, and buried. It was only three days later when things started to change. Mary Magdalene, John and Peter found the stone rolled away and the tomb empty. But then, Jesus began to appear alive. Jesus appeared first to Mary Magdalene, then the disciples. Thomas wasn't there when Jesus, after his resurrection, visited the other disciples. Thomas wasn't sure Jesus was raised from the dead until Jesus appeared to him personally (John 20). Then later,

Thomas and over five hundred people testified they had seen Jesus alive. But for awhile, none of them were certain. God knows about our sometimes not being sure about things.

One of the common uncertainties for young people is whether or not they're a Christian. You might find yourself questioning your own salvation. You might think, I think I'm saved, I went forward at the altar; or I think I'm saved, I was baptized as an infant; or I think I'm saved I go to a Christian church. I think I'm saved, I think I'm saved, I think I'm saved. If you're uncertain, it's okay to say so. But when we delve into the Bible we notice, that it was when the disciples received the Holy Spirit they became certain (John 20:22). The Holy Spirit is the person who changes us from being uncertain to certain. So okay, let me put it to you another way. In history-"in the olden days"-a king used a unique seal to prove orders were truly from Him The king's seal prevented people from falsely representing the heart of the king and his orders. A similar example is with United States currency. Paper bills have changed over the course of American history to prevent counterfeiting. Many different markings are on the bills. Some of the most important ways to tell authentic US currency from fake US currency, are that the real paper bills are made of cotton and linen which gives the bills a unique texture. The bills also have various red and blue fibers therein. Finally, there's also some raised printing, distinct coloring of numbers, other raised printing, and microprinting. All of these features make it easier to tell fake from real. In a similar way, God gives us the Holy Spirit as a marking so that He can tell we are His. But God also gives us the Holy Spirit so We can tell we are His. The Bible says that the Holy Spirit is a deposit, guaranteeing our inheritance. God wants us to be able to put thoughts of insecurity of whether or not we'll be saved to rest. A guarantee is something that is certain and without doubt. The Holy Spirit indwelling us guarantees that one day we will be in heaven with the Lord.

As a young person, I had a clear experience of the Holy Spirit when I was born again and said, "Yes" to the Lord.. It is a day I will never forget. From that moment on, the Holy Spirit dwelled in me, I had the seal from our King. I want to be very clear here, we can be aware of the Holy Spirit, we can be around Him and even sense Him, but us being around Him is not the same as Him being in us. Once I was born again and the Holy Spirit dwelled in me I didn't question my salvation. The Bible says that our questioning of whether or not we're in Christ can be silenced. We can be certain we're in Christ because the Holy Spirit lives in us. Jesus emphasized that following Him could be seen by a changed life. Jesus said, "You call me Lord Lord but you don't do what I say".(Luke 6:46, John 14:23). He was saying that there are certain actions that are like the particular markings on US currency, substantiate we're real and not fake, we've made Jesus Lord of our life. We don't need to be worrying about whether we're saved—we know it beyond a shadow of doubt! We're the real deal, we're sealed.

Further Study: 2Corinthians 1:18-22, 5:1-10

The Comforter and Warmth in the House
Understanding the Holy Spirit

> *But very truly I tell you it is for your good that I am going away. Unless I go away, the Comforter will not come to you; but if I go, I will send him to you.*
> *John 16:7 (Jesus)*

The comfort of a hug and the warmth of a wool blanket on a brisk, winter's night are a shadow of the comfort of the Holy Spirit. Another name for the Holy Spirit is Comforter. God is like a huge comforter, you know one of those Pottery Barn type comforters. Imagine spending a weekend at a log cabin in the woods surrounded by trees during a blizzard. Imagine you are snowed in and there's a blizzard raging outside. Imagine there's a fire crackling in the fireplace, and you just made it into the cabin and are so happy to be out of the storm. You've come here because of the exhaustion of your life. You enter the room and the room temperature is perfect, there are cups of warm tea and hot chocolate around and you see elite comforters. There are white fluffy beds with multiple cushy pillows. You barely get your shoes off and you fall into the bed. You cover yourself in the comforter and you just melt and you have a really deep, deep sleep. During your sleep you dream wonderful dreams of exhilaration and peace. The Holy Spirit is like that, giving rest and peace.

If you have believed on Jesus, if you have trusted Him with your life and taken Him as your savior, then you must know you have the comfort of a kind companion in your house. Now wait you say, only my mom and I live in our house and it's really lonely and my mom is always too tired to entertain and have company. Or you might be thinking, no one seems to like coming over to my house. Or maybe you are an only child and your house seems so quiet compared to your friends' houses. Or maybe even your dad blows up all the time and you're too embarrassed so you never invite anyone over. No matter what the reason is, if your house is a lonely place to be and if you have difficult things to endure, take heart, there's always company in your house and the Holy Spirit will comfort you.

The Holy Spirit comforts us during the storms of life. Even if there is a blizzard blowing, the Lord can wrap you in reassurance. The Holy Spirit inside the believer gives encouragement to endure through the storms of life when they come. The Holy Spirit is like the warmth of embers in the fireplace allowing one to go on in spite of even frigid temperatures. The Holy Spirit is comforting in a world demonstrating hostility to God. The Holy Spirit Comforter empowers the Lord's followers to be able to endure and to do difficult things. God does not promise a life free from storms, but He does give believers comfort through the Holy Spirit during the storms of life so that we can make it through.

Further Study: John 14:15-31, John 15:26, John 16:7, Romans 5:3-5, Romans 15:13

Cleansing Agent-Sanctification
Understanding the Holy Spirit

> .... *saved through the sanctifying work of the Spirit. 2Thessalonians 2:13-14*
> ...*called to be his holy people. 1Corinthians 1:2*

So now we know some foundational things about the Holy Spirit. But what are His functions? The author of Thessalonians states that the Spirit is the One through whom sanctification occurs. The word sanctification is a huge word. Sanctification is like a cleansing agent. Have you got some Brillo pads, some SOS, or how about some Tilex and Comet? Do you have a vacuum cleaner and maybe just some muscle power? Dear friends, Do you clean your house and your bathroom? Truth is some of you don't, but you should.

I'll never forget the day I went into my son's bedroom and I mean it was a total pigsty. Truth is I could hardly believe it. I had no idea it was such a disaster. But the really odd thing was his friend was in there. I don't know how two people could even be standing in there if you know what I mean. So there I am standing in the hall and I am telling my son to clean up the mess. And my son looks back at me and says how it's perfectly fine and good. And his friend joins in and talks about how he is perfectly fine in this room and he doesn't see any mess in there. And I said, "What are you kidding me, you can't see it?"

Truth is, it's the same way with us, we are messy on the inside and we need to get cleaned up and sometimes we just don't see it. The Holy Spirit is concerned with our inner core and our motives. The Holy Spirit wants to clean up not only what we do, but also more importantly our driving motivations for why we are doing certain things that are not helpful. Sometimes we can't see that we need a little cleaning up and sometimes we haven't even had emotional space in our lives to understand why we are doing certain things. But we shouldn't be afraid of the process. The Holy Spirit is there to help us. He is for us. He is for you.

The Holy Spirit is concerned with the interior work of our hearts and minds; He is concerned with the work of purification in our lives. You should not be surprised or discouraged if you make some mistakes. We all make mistakes. We all need love and forgiveness. If we get corrected it means we are loved. The Spirit does not only love us, but He corrects us so that we can grow up and be cleaned up. We all feel good after we've had a warm shower and are dressed in clean clothes. Clean bathrooms and clean bedrooms are good too! Likewise, being cleansed by the Holy Spirit might be a little painful at times, but in the end, it is good to be cleaned on the inside.

Further Study: John 2:12-25, Colossians 3, 1John 2:15-17

Omnipotence-Unlimited Power Supply

Understanding the Holy Spirit

> *Do not get drunk on wine, which leads to debauchery. Instead, be filled with the Spirit. Ephesians 5:18*
>
> *Jesus replied, "You are in error because you don't know the Scriptures or the power of God." Matthew 22:29*
>
> *His father, Zechariah was filled with the Holy Spirit and prophesied: "Praise be to the Lord the God of Israel, because he has come to his people and redeemed them. He has raised up a horn of salvation for us in the House of his servant David." Luke 1:67-6*

Zechariah was the father of John the Baptist. Zechariah had been silenced because he doubted the power of God to give him a son after his wife Elizabeth had been infertile for so many years. At the miraculous birth of his son John, Zechariah got his voice back and immediately was filled with the Holy Spirit prophesying meaning he proclaimed things about God. Zechariah saw God's power in the miraculous birth of his son and the power of the Holy Spirit welled up into him praising God for the coming Messiah. In another instance, Jesus was talking to the Sadducees who didn't believe in the resurrection. Jesus explained to the Sadducees that their error was that they didn't believe in the power of God. God is powerful, He is omnipotent meaning all powerful.

When I was parenting my four sons, I always enjoyed when it came time for science fair. I really liked helping with the science experiments and understanding the inner workings of how God made the world. One year we did a project demonstrating what happens when you add an acid to a base. When baking, one often adds baking soda into the recipe to react with an acidic ingredient or adding baking powder which already includes both an acid and a base. This mixture of acid plus base results in the formation of carbon dioxide causing baked goods to rise. Similarly, God wants us to be filled with power to prophesy which means to proclaim His word. He wants us to "rise" to the great calling we have in Jesus. For those of us who confess with our mouths Jesus is the Christ and believe in our hearts Jesus is Lord, the good news is we have God the Holy Spirit living inside of us. While God is omnipotent-meaning all powerful, we have the indwelling Holy Spirit who gives us spiritual power allowing us to "rise" above seemingly impossible obstacles. The Holy Spirit dwells in all who are saved and thus all Christians have access to the power of the Holy Spirit to evangelize and disciple.

We want to be filled with the Spirit. Some people who are Christians are living defeated lives and they need revival. Living a victorious Christian life is possible for all Christians. Examples of empowered living are seen throughout the New Testament. The filling of the Holy Spirit empowered the Apostle Peter to stand up and preach Christ in the midst of having been brought into captivity by the religious leaders of his day. The religious leaders were bothered because Peter was openly preaching about Jesus and His resurrection. They also were bothered because Peter had healed a crippled beggar. Listen, these leaders thought they weren't going to have any problems anymore because they had killed Jesus. They thought it was over, but now soon after Jesus' death, Peter was filled with the same power as Jesus. Peter was empowered to heal and to teach and to preach. This Peter who weeks before had denied he was a friend of Jesus, was changed and carrying on Jesus' work.

The Spirit is the electricity of the Christian life. The Good News is we have a supply of power to fuel our lives, we just need to stay connected to the source, remaining close to Him. As we stay close to the Lord, we find ourselves in line with the Spirit of God and our faith is resting on God's power not on human intellect. God has wonderful things in store for us who love Him. Dear Ones, God has many spiritual gifts He gives His children as He sees fit. The Lord teaches us to desire the greater gifts and that the Lord gives gifts joyfully.

Further Study: Micah 3:8, Luke 1:15,41,67; Acts 2:4, 4:7-33, 5:3, 9:17, 13:9, 13:52; 1Cor 2:6-16.

Further Study on Spiritual Gifts: Matthew 7:7-12, 1 Cor 12-14, Ephesians 1:3-14, 4:1-16

Further Study on Power: Matt 22:29, Matt 24:30, Mk 5:30, Mk 12:24, Lk 4:14, Lk 4:36, Lk 5:17, Lk 6:19, Lk 8:46, Lk 24:49, Acts 1:8, Acts 3:12, Acts 6:8, Acts 19:20, Rom 15:13-19, 1Cor 1:17-24, 1Cor 2:4-5, 1Cor 4:19-20, 1Cor 5:4, 2Cor 4:7, 2Cor 6:7, 2Cor 10:4, 2Cor 12:9, Eph 1:19-21, Eph 3:7-20, Phil 3:10-21, Col 1:11, 1Th 1:5, 2Th 1:11, 2Tim 1:7-8, 2Tim 3:5, 2Peter 1:3

Omnipresence
He Does Not Play Hide and Seek, He Plays Seek and Find, He is Willing To Be Known
Understanding the Holy Spirit

Where can I go from your Spirit? Where can I flee from your presence? Psalm 139:7

You will seek me and find me when you seek me with all your heart. Jeremiah 29:13

Don't you know that you yourselves are God's temple and that God's Spirit dwells in your midst? 1Corinthians 3:16

As we learn to walk with the Lord we ask Him to make Himself real to us, and to fill us with His Presence. We also ask Him to help us to really experience Him in such a way that we begin to realize He is the best thing and His Presence is the most important thing we want. In the Old Testament, the priests who served in the temple were the only ones who had access to the Spirit on a daily basis. At certain times in the Old Testament, the presence of God could be seen in the form of a cloud. Sometimes the cloud got so thick that the priests could not see clearly to perform their tasks. But also in the Old Testament sometimes the people would see the cloud as well. When the people saw the cloud at the entrance to the tent of meeting they would worship the Lord. Also when the Israelites were freed from the Egyptians, the cloud pillar led the people by day, and by night there was a pillar of fire. But the people didn't have the Presence constantly like we do today. If you are in Christ, the Good News is God Has Moved into your house. He lives with you now. God the Spirit, is omnipresent, He is with us everywhere we go because He resides in us so that all believers can be having conversations with God anytime.

If you are in Christ, then the Holy Spirit is always with you. Hebrews 13:5 says, "Never will I leave you, never will I forsake you." Now this does not mean that everyone has this companionship. Some people have the Spirit and some people do not. The Holy Spirit does not reside in everyone. It's important to get to know people. In the meantime, realize that Him being with you is not based on whether you feel Him or not. You must take Him at His word, His promise. He has promised it. It is true. Now, there are times when we definitely can sense the manifest presence of the Spirit. Just like in the Old Testament, the Israelites could experience God by His Presence in the cloud pillar and the pillar of fire, so too today, we can detect God's Presence with us. But whether His Presence is detectable or not, He is with you.

We want a life where we transparently say, "We need God". We must accept that it is our inadequacies that drive us to Him. The imperfect in our life makes our hearts seek Him out until we find Him. Some of us have experienced the backside of evil and because of that we long for Him. And so we seek Him and we find the complete person of Jesus. In Jesus we are made complete, we are made whole. Having been completed in Him, we follow Him, and we live lives of obedience. We are filled with the Holy Spirit and thus bring His presence with us in the world and have the God adventure life that He alone has crafted in advance for us.

Sometimes we don't feel the presence of the Lord, but it is a lie to believe He is not there. We take God at His word. God is a faithful friend who can be found for those who are willing to seek. He loves for us to spend time with Him and get to know Him better. It is in this pursuit of God, living an active life of walking by faith, and following an adventurous God filled life that we find our wholeness, our completion. God does not play hide and seek, God plays seek and find. God is delighted when we seek Him and He loves to show Himself to us, He loves to be found.

Further Study: Deuteronomy 31:8; Matthew 28:20; John 2:19-21, 14:16-17; Acts 2:1-13, Acts 4-especially 4:8 & 4:31, Acts 13:52, 16:34, Rom 15:14, 1Corinthians 2:6-16, 3:16-17, 6:19-20, Ephesians 5:18, Hebrews 11:6

Further Study on Presence: Exodus 13:21-33, 14:19-24, 25:30, 28:30, 33:15-19, 34:29-35, 35:13, 40:34-38; Lev 9:24, 10:2; Num 4:7, 10:11-12; 1Kings 8:10-12, Luke 1:19, John 8:38, Acts 2:28, 10:33, 1 Thessalonians 3:9

Special Thanks to David Swarbrick Jr., Rob Harrell, and Ross Parsley

Omniscience
He Knows What Is True And He Is Truth
Understanding the Holy Spirit

Jesus said, "And I will ask the Father, and he will give you another Counselor to be with you forever—The Spirit of Truth...." John 14:16-17a

Jesus said, "But the Counselor, the Holy Spirit, whom the Father will send in my name, will teach you all things and will remind you of everything I have said to you". John 14:26

Jesus said, "But when he, The Spirit of Truth comes, he will guide you into all truth. He will not speak on his own; he will speak only what he hears, and he will tell you what is yet to come. John 16:13

The Lord does not look at the things people look at. People look at the outward appearance, but the Lord looks at the heart. 1Samuel 16:7

Until we all reach unity in the faith and in the knowledge of the Son of God and become mature, attaining to the whole measure of the fullness of Christ. Eph 4:13

God wants all people to be saved and to come to a knowledge of the truth. 1Timothy 2:4

Dear Ones, there are certain kids that are known as "know it alls". When I was a kid, we called that kid, Miss Information. Miss Information could always be counted on to explain things to you whether or not you wanted to hear what she had to say. There are many people today willing to share their knowledge with you. When we go to the bank, the teller lets us know how much money we have in our bank account. When we go to the doctor, he lets us know what our diagnosis is and will explain to us what we must do to get well. When we go to school, our teachers tell us what we must do to pass the tests.

In the Bible, we learn through many Scriptures that the Holy Spirit is omniscient, He knows everything. Dear Ones, not only does the Holy Spirit know everything, but just like the teller, the doctor, and the teacher; so too, the Holy Spirit is happy to give His knowledge and wisdom out freely to those who ask for it. Jesus called the Holy Spirit the Counselor and The Spirit of Truth. The Holy Spirit counsels us by helping us understand what is true, what is real. Sometimes we make a mistake and believe a lie we've been told. The Holy Spirit has an active role in teaching us truth and reminding us of what the Bible says. It is written in James 1:5, If any of you lacks wisdom, he should ask God, who gives generously…and it will be given to him. God desires for you to ask for wisdom. He wants you to know Him and grow in understanding. Having personal knowledge of God aides in understanding all of life's complexities. God's prophet Hosea lamented that the Israelites were not as strong as they could have been because they didn't possess knowledge (Hosea 4:6a). Knowledge and understanding strengthens people. This is why there is the saying that knowledge is power. Not only does the Lord have knowledge to help us, but knowing God comforts us because we know God wins in the end. The Holy Spirit Counselor reminds us God has wonderful things prepared for us who love Him-far greater than what we can imagine (1Cor 2:9-10).

But there also is a flip side to the knowledge of God. The author of Samuel says that God looks on man's heart. The Holy Spirit knows what's in our heart. He knows if we're scheming against others, or working to bless and enrich others. He knows if we're being kind and sharing or stingy and greedy. The Holy Spirit knows if we're helping others to know God, or if we are hindering others from coming to God. Because we understand that the Holy Spirit knows everything, we should fear the Lord. This fear of the Lord is a fear that brings us to a place of friendship with God because over time the Holy Spirit works to purify the motives of our hearts and we obey Him because we know He knows what we're up to!

Further Study: Exodus 31:3; 2Chronicles 1:10-12; Proverbs 1:1-7; 2:5-6, 12:1, 15:7,14, 17:27, 22:12, 24:4-5; Isaiah 11:2-9; Jer 3:15; Dan 1:17, 2:21, 5:12; Luke 1:77; Mat 13:11; John 14:15-31, 16:5-16; Rom 10:2; 1Corinthians 1:5; 2:6-16, 6:6-16, 8:10-11, 12:8, 13:2,8, 14:6; 2Corinthians 2:14, 10:5; Philippians1:9; Colossians 1:9-10; 1 Tim 6:20

Don't Be a Bed Head! Get Up! Plan For Your Future
The Big Picture

Go to the ant, you sluggard, consider its ways and be wise! It has no commander, overseer or ruler, yet it stores its provisions in summer and gathers its food at harvest. How long will you lay there, you sluggard? When will you get up from your sleep? Proverbs 6:6-9

But work, doing something useful, so that you have something to share with those in need. Ephesians 4:28

So a very small thing, an ant, has a lot to teach us. The tiny ant is considering the big picture instead of just the tiny little details contained in a single day. The ant has in his sight the overall picture. So the ant in the verse above is planning a year out. In the summer it spends its time storing provisions and then at harvest it gathers its food. Dear Ones, the ant does not eat all of its food during the summer, it puts things away for later. This applies to your life as a teenager or a young adult. You need to be looking ahead and beginning to understand what your life is going to look like for the year. What subjects will you be focusing on? Will you spend more time in prayer? Will you be working on gaining skills to play an instrument? What spiritual gift do you want to grow in? Will you try to get certified as a referee? Will you apply for a summer job? Are you going to be taking driver's education this year? Are you going to try and read the entire New Testament? Do you want to apply for an internship? Do you want to go on a short-term mission trip to explore the idea of missions? Just what are your goals for the year? It is always good to set aside some time annually to think about what you are really going to work towards and get out of the mindset of only focusing on the micro daily things. If you don't see the big picture, then you may not have what you need at the end of the year like satisfaction in personal and spiritual growth and development.

The second thing we learn from the proverb of the ant is that the ant does not have a ruler, and yet on his own accord he is ruling his own life, getting up and setting up his own goals. This is so important because some of us have parents who have time for us and some of us don't. Some of us have lost a parent due to death or neglect. No matter what our circumstance, one can be like the ant that gets up and gets on with life becoming master of himself and still planning for its future.

The third thing we learn from the proverb of the ant is to not be lazy, but instead be productive so that you will have a harvest. Don't be a bed head. Get up! Get out of bed! If you don't plant, if you don't invest in your life, then later in your life, you won't have resources to draw on. You need to make the most of the opportunities you have to develop yourself while you have the chance to do so. It's just a good principle to understand that you need to get up in the morning and get moving and stop lazing the day away.

So I am trying to get you to look at the forest for a while and not the trees. You have to step away and look at the bigger overall picture of your life. The main thing is the main thing, and the minor things are the minor things. At least once during the year take time to focus on the major plans and not the minor plans of your life. Then when the year is done, see if you met some of your major goals for the year.

Further Study: Genesis 2:2-3, Genesis 2:15, Genesis 3:13-19, 1Thessalonians 4:11-12, 1Thessalonians 5:1-14, 2Thessalonians 3:6-15

Live With Purpose, Live On Mission
The Big Picture

> *Go therefore and make disciples of all nations, baptizing them in the name of the Father and of the Son and of the Holy Spirit. Matthew 28:19*
>
> *Cornelius, God has heard your prayer and remembered your gifts to the poor. Acts 10:31*
>
> *For you know the grace of our Lord Jesus Christ, that though he was rich, yet for your sake he became poor, so that through his poverty you might become rich. 2Corinthians 8:9*

Dear Ones, we serve a God of commission and mission. The Lord commissions us as men and women of God to step up and be spiritual parents to many lost and hurting among us and around us. It doesn't matter how old we are, all of us can be a part of the Lord's work in the world. We have a great calling. If you have taken time to be healed and you're moving on toward living a missional life then join with me in telling people about Jesus. This can be done in a number of ways such as discipling others, ministering to the poor, working in the youth department of your local church, helping plant churches overseas, or even ministering to an unreached people group.

God is so kind, He gives us the great honor of being His ambassador to the world. God has given us the example of Jesus. Jesus demonstrates to us how to live a God-centric life instead of a self-centric life. Jesus' example is that He left the comforts of heaven in order to serve. Although Jesus was rich, He became poor for our sakes. He left heaven behind and came to earth so that we could know God. We can be like God, when we serve those who don't yet know God, or when we serve those of a lower socioeconomic group who have not had the benefits we have grown up with. When we serve the poor, the orphans, and the foreigners, it is then that we become acquainted with our Lord more intimately because it is then that we begin to know Jesus in His sufferings. Our Lord has a heart for the hurting as well as a heart for those who do not yet know about Jesus. To begin to live like Jesus is a great privilege. We can minister to others bringing the Good News, help those in poverty, help heal others, and bring freedom and light to those spiritually in bondage. When we minister to others and we find our purpose, it is then that we have joy.

Further Study: Isaiah 61:1, Luke 4:18

The Blind Ref-Play With Heart
The Big Picture

Never be lacking in zeal, but keep your spiritual fervor, serving the Lord.
Romans 12:11

So I was at a soccer game the other night. We didn't have linesmen and the center ref could not see to make appropriate calls. For the sake of argument let's just say he did not intend to miss calls but that he couldn't see and that he really missed some important ones. It was in fact easy to give him grace because he was put into an impossible situation anyway of having to do three people's jobs—an unjust situation to be put into. Our kids were trying really hard to win the game but the game was close so the calls now get to a level where they can make or break the outcome. If the game were not close it wouldn't matter, but because the game is close, it suddenly matters, suddenly the unjustness of our kids trying so hard and not having linesmen becomes more glaringly real. I falter and I make a call for the ref, "Corner kick", I say. I do not attack the ref but I do loudly state my call. But wait, I have forgotten, I am not the ref. It takes me nearly a day to get over the humiliation of my becoming the ref from the sidelines. I vicariously was reffing the game. I have thought about getting certified as a ref but I never have done it. I have always coached because I loved doing that but reffing would just be a side, it would never be my main dish. It is not because I am not able to ref, it is because I don't care enough and perhaps I am a little lazy. But this guy he is not lazy. He is out there reffing even though he looks like he is nearing seventy years old. He is using every opportunity to keep fit and have fun in spite of people vicariously reffing from the sidelines. He acts as though he doesn't even hear me.

So why was the blind ref given to us? Why did the ref make the call for a goal kick instead of a corner kick, so clearly the incorrect call? Why did he call off sides and take away our goal when clearly we were onside? Sometimes, blind refs are stretched beyond their limits, like in this situation. When we see unjustness we should work for justice because significant people are always looking to do what is right. A good way to respond to the injustice in the above scenario is not to vicariously become the ref on the sidelines, but the answer here is to get linesmen. Linesmen would help the center ref do his job in a more just manner.

Yet in spite of the unjustness of the situation and the need to work for justice, why was the blind ref given to us? The blind ref calls deep within our souls to play for the love of the game. Does sport really matter? Do we care deeply enough to go even deeper and find the heart in our play? In the second half of that game, we were behind but we began to find our heart. We kept firing, we kept attacking the net, and we began to finally find our heart. We didn't obtain victory but we grew some. The blind ref forced us to dig deeper to really question ourselves, to believe on a deeper level. Maybe we weren't dreaming big enough dreams, maybe we weren't trying hard enough, and maybe we didn't believe enough. Could we overcome not only our opposition, could we overcome our opposition plus the twelfth man; the opposition plus an unjust situation? People who have played sports long enough know that sometimes there is a twelfth man to overcome and sometimes there are unjust situations to overcome. To deny this truth is to deny the reality of the game. However those who love the game also believe in the human heart. Those who love the game set their sights on greater heights. They set their sights higher knowing that if they gave everything, if they tried harder, if they dug deeper in fact then, even the twelfth man and an unjust situation could not stop them. Because people who play with heart can overcome all odds, even the twelfth man, even injustice.

Dear friends, God wants us in the game playing with engaged hearts, hearts that are passionate for Him and His purposes in the world. A passionate heart that is sold out to Jesus can overcome all odds. So fight the good fight of faith with zeal. Play with heart.

Further Study: 1Samuel 15-2 Samuel 24 (The life of David), 1Samuel 13:14, Acts 13:22

Walk By Faith And Don't Forget To Exercise
The Big Picture

> *Abram believed the Lord and he credited it to him as righteousness. Genesis 15:6*
> *Without faith it is impossible to please God, because anyone who comes to him must believe that he exists and that he rewards those who earnestly seek him. Hebrews 11:6*

Walking by faith is the application of knowledge and understanding. What does this mean? Dear friends, many people are more interested in knowing about God, rather than following God in faith and obedience. Walking by faith is not like taking a knowledge test, rather it is more like taking a skills test. When you take a skills test you check to see if you can apply what you know to specific challenging problems. To *only know about God*, means you are not following Him by faith. The person who is a follower of Jesus is willing to cooperate with God, to have God's attitudes that He says to have. To follow God means as you learn who God is,

183

you begin to walk in the knowledge you have. God is a covenantal God and He has promises for His people who follow Him. *To walk by faith is to apply His promises to your life and to believe them for your life. It is to stake your life on the foundation of His promises.*

How do we live a life of application? Did you read a Scripture that encouraged your heart? Then believe and thank the Lord for that Scripture. Do you need direction for your life? Proverbs 3:5,6 says to commit your way to Him and He will direct your path. Then believe in faith He will direct you as you go forward and thank Him in advance that you know He will direct your path in the future. Thanking Him in advance for what He will do in the future because He has promised it and you have found Him to be trustworthy is one example of how you can exercise your faith, building upon the foundation of His trustworthy promises.

Exercising to stay in shape takes work and effort. Similarly, spiritual exercise requires spiritual work. Do not be lazy about doing the spiritual work required for growth. Steel your mind as a soldier of Christ to live by faith. If God has made a promise in His word, then live by faith and actively depend on His promise. You must move forward. Sitting still is not exercising your faith. Get up and move. Move on, continue doing the Lord's work, apply the Lord's words to your life, and live according to the future reality promised even though you have not yet obtained it. Walk by faith and don't forget to exercise.

Further Study: Matt 19:29-30, Matt 28:19-20, 1Cor 3:10-15, 2Cor 5:9-15, Phil 3:12

Working For Justice
The Big Picture

Hate evil, love good; maintain justice in the courts. Amos 5:15
God executes justice every morning. Zephaniah 3:5
Do you question my Justice: Are you able to quell wicked men? Job 38-41

Dear Ones, God does not want someone falsely put into prison for murder if the person did not murder. Conversely, God wants the real murderers put into prison so that they are not wandering about seeking others to kill. He wants justice so that people have freedom, peace, and the ability to live a quiet lifestyle.

I am calling you to work for justice. If evil is having free reign then you must work to bring justice and work to bring the kingdom of God into the situation. God wants justice. True justice is where truth reigns and evil is punished. You maybe can't do everything, but maybe you can do something. You might not be able to prevent all evil, but you might be able to prevent some. Be prayerful. Stay alert. Start with a small thing like standing up for someone who is being treated unkindly. Stand up for someone who is being gossiped about and whose name is being slandered. Refuse to listen to it and refuse to gossip yourself. Start with that small commitment to justice and God who sees your faithfulness will entrust larger things to you in the future.

What God does call us to do is to work for justice and to enlarge His kingdom, not enlarge our own kingdoms. He calls us to set captives free and bring light to the blind. God wants to stop evildoers who hurt and harm the innocent and vulnerable. James reminds us especially to care for and look after orphans and widows (James 1:27). Jesus promises condemnation for those whose life is characterized by unfettered evil. My friend, when you see a terrorist, let's just say this, if he escapes without being caught, it is not over. No, it is not over until judgment day my friend, where Jesus promised to separate the wheat from the tares-then there will be weeping and gnashing of teeth. God is not happy when evil is given free reign and justice is lacking. He wants justice, and He wants people, especially the vulnerable to be protected (Proverbs 6:17b, 21:15).

As you grow in your faith you will learn to love justice and desire it more and more. You will tolerate evil less and be sickened by evil when you become wrapped up in bringing God's kingdom on earth. Many Christians rightly serve in our legal system to incarcerate the violent, while others rightly are working to free from prison the wrongly condemned. Other Christians of noble character are trying to free the sex-trafficked or addicted, while others are working to protect the rights of Christians in our society. We all need to have a divine dissatisfaction when we see people being treated unjustly. May the Lord utilize you to bring His justice.

Further Study: Psalm 45:7, Amos 5:15, Matthew 15:19, Mark 3:4, John 3:20

Being Faithful, Have High Fidelity

The Big Picture

> *"The Lord, the Lord, the compassionate and gracious God, slow to anger, abounding in love and faithfulness. Exodus 34:6*
>
> *You have neglected the more important matters of the law—justice, mercy, and faithfulness. Matthew 23:23*

Dear Ones, God values fidelity. God's character abounds in faithfulness, it's just who He is. As our faithful God, the Lord is present for us and available to help us. God understands our need for light and direction and He is faithfully present for us when we call upon Him. Not only is God consistently present for us, but God is also for us, hoping for us and has His arms outstretched toward us. As we experience God's faithful, covenantal love for us, then we learn how to return love for God with faithfulness to Him. What a comfort to know it is as though God is "coaching our team". Now just because He is for us that does not mean He is for everything that we do! God faithfully corrects us, and He also faithfully collects us when we fall. He collects us off the floor if needed, but his correction can steady us and keep us from falling. God being for us is like having a coach who wants us to get rid of our "ineffective plays" and wants us to replace them with more "effective plays". God being for us means He wants our growth, but He hangs in there with us when we misstep.

In Numbers 12:7, Moses was complimented by God as "being faithful in all my house." What a joy to be complimented by God! King David praised God in 2Samuel 22 that he was able to keep the ways of the Lord and not turn from God nor God's decrees. Ruth, faced with widowhood, refused to depart from Naomi and was heralded as a woman of noble character. These faithful people serve as examples to us. A heart that is first and foremost faithful to the Lord, responds by living out faithfully to his family and community. A faithful person understands that he has certain relationships of significance and he also has certain duties. A faithful parent and a faithful child comes to his home every day. Family relationships require consistent presence just like our relationship with the Lord requires consistent presence. If a stereo system has high fidelity it means that the reproduced sound is very faithful to its original. It means it does not meander from the original sound. Likewise, God wants us to be people who have high fidelity, to highly resemble Him. We are to be faithful to our master, Jesus, faithfully follow Him, becoming like Him in faithfulness. The Lord beckons us to be faithful to Him in the same way He is faithful to us, remaining present with the Lord and being for the Lord in all of our relationships. As we learn to be faithful to Him, we then overflow in faithfulness to our families and communities.

Further Study: Numbers 12:7; Deut 7:9; Deut 32:4; Ruth; 1 Sam 2:9, 35; 2 Sam 22:21-30, Ps 25:10, Ps 31:23; Ps 78:8,37; Ps 85:8; Ps 86:2; Ps 97:10; Matt 25:21-23; Rom 12:12; 1Cor 4:17; Eph 6:21; 1Tim 3:2; Rev 19:11

Knowing the Lord's Will
The Big Picture

> *If we live, we live for the Lord; and if we die, we die for the Lord. So whether we live or die, we belong to the Lord. Romans 14:8*
>
> *"Whoever does the will of my father in heaven is my brother and sister and mother." Matthew 12:50 (Jesus)*
>
> *You know you will receive an inheritance from the Lord as a reward. It is the Lord Christ you are serving. Colossians 3:24*

The questions are mostly over now and you have accepted Jesus and His Lordship over your life. You are practicing listening for what He says to you. He shapes your attitudes and your thoughts. As you are listening to Him, He tells you things to do. You try to do what He tells you to do. This is doing the Lord's will. Listen, people worry about fleeces, and specific revelation, but the most important thing is that you practice doing the multiplicity of things in His word that He has already revealed. It's like this: Imagine that you are a student of piano. Students first learn the fundamentals and then they learn simple songs to play. Once they have mastered the basic fundamentals of piano, then as they mature they can eventually play more complex pieces. You won't need to know how to play Bach until you can play simple songs.

Things like putting out fleeces and specific revelation is like playing the complex pieces on the piano. The necessary thing is to concentrate on the known will of God. In the early days in the life of a young Christian, ones who want to grow in leadership must continue to follow Jesus, doing all that He says to do. God gives special divine guidance as it is needed. God knows what wisdom and guidance you need and you should ask for wisdom whenever you need it, He gives liberally to those who ask for it, but there already is extensive revealed guidance. God's call to all Christians is to love God by making disciples. God's call is to treasure the things that God treasures, living for the unseen instead of the seen. Keep your focus on making your heart to be like God's heart. Where your treasure is, there your heart will be also. Treasure the things of God. Do justice, love mercy and practice faithfulness. Do the work of an evangelist and disciple people. Care for orphans and widows and be kind to the poor. Live your life to the Lord and He will reward you with His presence. Sow generously into the Lord's work and you will produce a harvest in due season. All of this amounts to the known will of God and covers the majority of what all young Christians need to know to grow and to live their life well.

Further Study: Matthew 5,6,7, Matthew 28:18-20, Matthew 10: 41; 2Cor 9:6, Revelation 22:12

Training For the Race-The Top of the World
The Big Picture

> *Have nothing to do with godless myths and old wives' tales; rather, train yourself to be godly. 1Timothy 4:7*
>
> *Everyone who competes in the games goes into strict training. They do it to get a crown that will not last, but we do it to get a crown that will last forever. 1Corinthians 9:25*

Athletes come from all around the world to compete in the Olympic games. The training regimen of all these athletes are different according to the sport they compete in, however the diligence required to compete is formidable. Not just anyone is allowed to compete. In order to be afforded the honor of competing in the Olympic games, your country must choose you to compete. In order to get to the highest level of competition one must first win at the lower levels. If one competes and wins at the local level, then one is moved on to regional competition, then state competition, and finally national competition. The winner of the national competition, then moves on to compete internationally in the Olympic games. To be an Olympian is to be at the top of the world so to speak. To get to the top requires hours and hours of grueling training. It is not for the faint of heart.

Paul, the writer of Corinthians encourages us to run our "faith race" as though we were running to get the top prize. While Paul freely acknowledges that athletes win prizes, he remarks that our prize is a crown that will endure forever. We are not working for a temporal reward but an eternal reward and because of this Paul mastered his body rather than being mastered by his body. Paul mastered his body through training, training his body to do the things that he wanted it to do. It is as though Paul is saying that like marathoners train for races, so too; those who want to grow and be mature must train themselves to productive Gospel work. So, the big picture of your life, is to work as unto the Lord, pleasing the Lord, and living to advance the Gospel in the world. Live for heaven and do the things that are profitable. Remember training takes the investment of time and discipline. You will reap what you sow. If you put yourself into training, you can reach Olympic heights, you will be on "top of the world" in God's eyes.

Further Study: 2Sam 22:35, Ps 144:1, Micah 4:3, Matt 10:40-43, Eph 6:4, 1Tim 4:8, 2Tim 3:16

Racing To Win-"All In"
The Big Picture

I have fought the good fight, I have finished the race, I have kept the faith. 2Timothy 4:7

But Jael, picked up a tent peg and a hammer…drove the tent peg through his temple into the ground, and he died. Judges 4:21

One of my favorite histories recorded in the Bible is the account of when Deborah was ruling Israel. Deborah was a judge at the time and she worked well with others. Deborah had learned a great lesson-the lesson about partnerships. Deborah partnered with a man named Barak and a woman named Jael. At that time in history, Jabin, a governor of a region in the Promised Land, was oppressing the Israelites. The Israelites were being oppressed because the Israelites weren't being careful to do all that the Lord told them to do and thus they had gotten into a situation of bondage and not of freedom. At this time, many people were coming to Deborah with their problems and she helped people sort through their "issues". She was a judge and she had an official position in the Jewish community, she wasn't just meeting with people unofficially. She had authority as a judge, she was the spiritual leader of the nation.

Deborah had an office and informed Barak of what the Lord's plans were. Deborah had received vision from God and told Barak to take 10,000 men to battle at Mt. Tabor and the Lord would give Sisera, the leader of Jabin's army, into their hands. Listen the battle was the Lord's. The Lord was giving sight for winning the battle. Now Barak did go to battle, but because Deborah was so powerful, Barak insisted Deborah go with him into battle. As Barak moved into battle, God gave Sisera into the hand of the woman, Jael. Jael took a tent peg and hammered it into the head of Sisera, when he was asleep. Deborah led the way to victory by following the Lord and by teaming up with Jael and Barak to defeat King Jabin and Sisera. Dear friends, this is racing to win. Deborah's dynamic sight, represents victorious Christian living and killing evil. To be victorious in the Christian life one must be all in, with one's heart and mind focused on victory. But victory comes to those who are willing to form partnerships, work well with others, and be careful to do all that the Lord says to do. Most importantly you have to go for it and be "all in". You must see things through to the end. If you start something you must continue to the finish. Do not quit until the job you are doing is completely done. See things through to the end. Race to win, don't give up the marathon when you are at mile twenty-five, rather, determine to cross the finish line. Regardless of your place, run your race until its completion and then you will have personal victory for your race. Your race is the only race you can finish, so finish well.

Further Study: Lk 14:25-35, John 4:34, John 19:28-37, Acts 20:13-38, 2Cor 8:10-12, Gal 3:3

Taskmaster or Dream Giver-Living Under the Pressure of Expectation or Living With Expectation

The Big Picture

> When the Lord restored the fortunes of Zion, we were like those who dreamed. Our mouths were filled with laughter, our tongues with sounds of joy. Then it was said among the nations, "The Lord has done great things for them." Psalm 126:1-2

> Then I hated life, because what is done under the son is grievous to me, for all is vanity and a striving after wind. Ecclesiastes 2:17

Some teenagers are so gifted that they carry the burden of unachievable expectations. Because they are so gifted, everyone believes they are the man or woman, they are the one who can do it all, and they forget that the gifted teen needs to be cared for, nurtured, led, shepherded and guided. They need the investment of time just like any other teen. To carry an inflated expectation because you are gifted is a burden.

Dear Ones, pressuring children with expectations which are unobtainable is not the heart of God. Ever increasing pressure on a child builds up in a child's heart like a pressure cooker, which occasionally erupts into an explosion. God is not a taskmaster pressuring his children to unobtainable achievements. Instead, God the Father is the dream giver. God weaves into our hearts dreams to pursue and the capacity to believe for great things. God desires us to find the joy of freedom to pursue our dreams. God the dream giver has built certain things into our makeup that are the foundation for our dreams, but He gives freedom as to how we walk out that dream, and to make decisions about what dream to follow.

For those teens that carry a heavy load of expectation from their nuclear family, I have a few things to say to you. First, you need to be able to articulate to a couple of close friends that you feel pressure from your family. Not to drag your parents through the mud and disrespect them, but in order to live authentically you have to share with someone your experience. Second, because your parents do not give you the joy of choice, does not mean that God does not give you the joy of choice. Make sure you differentiate between the two. Third, God gives freedom for people to walk away from excessive expectation into the place of freedom in the Lord, but while you are still living at home you must be careful to obey your parents. Finding freedom within a pressure packed home is not impossible, but neither is it easy. To find freedom while living in a home of excessive expectation, do the following: first, tune into your heart…ask your heart, is this something I want to do or am I being pressured to do it? If you are feeling pressured by your parents, say to them without emotion, "I am feeling pressured which is cutting off my joy." Also let them know, "I would like more freedom to choose for myself." "I statements" are more effective than accusatory statements such as; "You are always pressuring me." If you are living in that pressure packed home, ask God to replace the pressure with a dream. If you can focus on the dream, then that will relieve some of the pressure you are living under.

On the other hand, if you are pressuring yourself excessively to live beyond your capacity, then cease striving and first learn just how to love and enjoy God. God wants to move you to the place where you live for Him, not for your parents, your coach, or even your friends. Living with your heart fully engaged in a dream that God has given you, brings both you and God great pleasure. If your heart is fully invested in living your life as to the Lord, you will then begin experiencing God not as a taskmaster who pressures you but the dream giver who frees you to pursue your dreams. He wants to move you to the place of release from expectation to the place of expecting great things from God. Playing for a dream prevents explosions and it allows you to play explosively. What you are dreaming of?

A last consideration is simply this: sometimes you have to walk away from something before you can walk toward it with your heart fully engaged. Walking away is always an option. When one walks away from something, the Lord will give you insight to walk towards something new or to come back later when you're ready. *Special thanks to David Swarbrick, Jr

Further Study: Gen 20, Gen 28:10-22, Gen 31:10-13, Gen 31:24, Gen 37:1-11, Gen 40-41, Judges 7, 1 Kings 3, Dan 2,4,7; Joel 2:28, Matt 1:20, Matt 2, Acts 2:17

20/20 Vision-Seeing Clearly

The Big Picture

"But solid food is for the mature, who by constant use have trained themselves to distinguish good from evil." Hebrews 5:14

Don't let anyone look down on you because you are young but set an example for the believers in speech, in conduct, in love, in faith and in purity. 1Timothy 4:12

Where there is no revelation, people cast off restraint. Proverbs 29:18

Having 20/20 vision is a great thing because it means you can see clearly. If you have poor vision and can't see you won't be able to get a license to drive a car. You will need someone to assist you for most of the time when you are venturing out of doors. Your choice of vocation may be limited. If you are blind it is a great hardship. Now I am not saying that one cannot compensate well or have a full life if they are blind. All I am saying is it is a challenge. Similarly, you start out, as a young Christian and you just don't know that much, so we might say you have imperfect vision of 40/40. But as you practice detecting what is from God and what is not from God, then your sight improves to 20/20. Everyone cannot see with the same clarity. The author of Hebrews states that increased acuity comes to ones who train and practice.

Also the author of Hebrews mentions that solid food is for the mature. When babies are born they only drink milk. Most babies don't start on solids until four to six months of age. They can't digest anything besides milk at the beginning of life. In the same way, if you are young in Christ, you cannot discern or understand everything. Don't be discouraged by this, instead determine in your mind and heart to keep learning from God what is good and what is not. You should not be looked upon as a Christian youth, but know that in Christ you can even set an example in your youth, even keeping such a devotion to God that your faith, purity and love will draw others to Christ. Your life will provide sight for others.

Without vision the people of God fall into sin, but God's vision for how to live brings life to His people. This means that the greatest vision of all is the vision that the Lord gives to His church in community. Vision is what ultimately encourages the body of Christ to do the Lord's work. So vision is excellent both physically as it lights one's path, and spiritually as it lights the path of the church's mission in the world.

Further Study: Daniel 5:12, Matthew 16:1-4, Luke 12:1-12, Luke 12:54-59

When Things Aren't Working, Give It Up!
The Big Picture

> *That is why a man leaves his father and mother and is united to his wife, and they become one flesh. Genesis 2:24*

> *Rather, we have renounced secret and shameful ways; we do not use deception, nor do we distort the word of God. On the contrary by setting forth the truth plainly we commend ourselves to everyone's conscience in the sight of God. 2Cor 4:2*

> *But the Jewish leaders incited the God-fearing women of high standing and the leading men of the city. They stirred up persecution against Paul and Barnabas, and expelled them from the region. Acts 13:50*

I grew up in a large family. I was the middle child of seven children. With such a large family there were a lot of needs and so we often went to garage sales, hunting for deals. As an adult, I have hosted garage sales. A common question that is asked at garage sales is, "Does this work?" It seems so obvious, but most of the time if an item doesn't work, then people don't want it. One time someone was shopping at my garage sale and the wife said to the husband, "You really need to stop buying things that don't work, we have an entire garage filled with things that don't work." We kind of smile to ourselves and wonder why it is that people are so silly. At what point do people learn their lesson, what does it take? If something doesn't work, it is more fruitful to ask questions, and seek a new way. Perhaps people are afraid of the unknown, but for me the unfruitful way is what I want to abandon quickly. For even if I falter on my way to finding the new way, I will be farther ahead than clinging to what I know doesn't work. In 1987, U.S. President Ronald Reagan boldly spoke to Gorbachev, "Tear down this wall." And the wall came down as a symbol of more freedom coming in the East.

194

Likewise Joshua in the battle of Jericho led the Israelites to silently march around Jericho for six days, then on the seventh day to march seven times around Jericho and shout. When the Israelites obeyed and gave a shout, then the wall came down. Listen, things that are in the way of God's kingdom advancing need to be taken down. When we have an ongoing problem we must ask ourselves if that tradition is of the Lord, do we need to abandon doing that which is not working and is not fruitful? Do we need to give it up?

There are problems that will present themselves in the Christian life. When a major problem is occurring, it is always good to ask if a change needs to be made. Is there a better way if we try something else? Sometimes we are just so comfortable living with things as they are and we want to hold onto our tradition or practice instead of letting things go that don't work, things that aren't bringing the kingdom. Sometimes we just can't see how silly we are being. We are like the man at the garage sale who keeps collecting broken things. He just can't see what he is doing wrong. If someone keeps trying to tell you something, then you might want to listen.

One common problem occurs when people try to start their marriage and they haven't really left home. They keep living in the same town they grew up in and their parents keep giving the newly married couple money and advice and meals and the young couple fails to learn to depend on each other. Now I am not saying it is not possible to live in the same town you grew up in, I am just saying it is necessary for young married couples to emotionally and physically replace the practice of depending on their parents and replace it with the practice of depending on their new spouse. If you are unable to do that living in the same town, then you might consider moving. All young couples have to learn to give up over dependence on their parents.

Another problem occurs when people do secret things. Anything that is done in secrecy needs to be brought to the light. If a family member or a church is doing secret things, then this needs to be discussed and examined and prayed about. Most often, secret activities just need to be given up, renounced, and replaced with the practice of being open and honest.

Finally, if someone is kicking you out, like Paul and Barnabas were kicked out, it is not wise to try and stay. It might be okay for a short, specific period of time, but it is not okay to stay and start a battle. Too many times when Christians have a beef against a leader they stay and speak against the leadership and start a church fight. If you oppose something your leadership is doing it would be better to leave quietly and not try to drag people out of a church with you. Give up trying to stay somewhere that you are getting kicked out of. A good historical account of a conspiracy is found in the book of 2Samuel. Absalom, the son of King David found himself at odds with his king, with his leader. Absalom got fifty men with him and began to form a coalition against his leader. Needless to say, the historical account does not end well for Absalom. Absalom was killed and the conspiracy failed. Proverbs says he who digs a pit will fall into it. Leave the scene quietly, leave rather than start a fight. After your case has been quietly shared with the leadership, and if the leadership of your church rejects your ideas, it is so much wiser to give it up, move on, and look for different people to work with, people who you are more comfortable serving under. If your leadership has a change of heart and invites you back, you have the option to return. You preserve yourself with peace.

Further Study: Joshua 5:13-6:27, 2Samuel 15-19:8, Luke 9:5, Acts 8:1-8, Acts 11:19-30, Acts 12:1-19, Acts 13:45-52, Acts 14:8-20, Acts 15:46-51, Acts 16:16-40

Being Given Up-Resolve the Cycle, Pass the Baton
The Big Picture

> It is good to grasp the one and not let go of the other. Whoever fears God will avoid all extremes. Ecclesiastes 7:18
>
> But as for me, it is good to be near God. I have made the Sovereign Lord my refuge; I will tell of all your deeds. Psalm 73:28

The saying "I was given up as a child" can bring up feelings of ambivalence or feelings of pain for ones who were adopted or placed into foster care as children. Sometimes these precious ones feel unloved because of their biological parents' failures. Unanswered questions might linger about why parents placed their child for adoption or into foster care, leaving young people with a desire to resolve the past. This being stuck in the past (for anyone who suffered any significant trauma as a child btw), causes people to cycle back through things. Humans desire to resolve their issues, and they cycle, and cycle, and cycle again until they get it right. The human heart cycles until it achieves victory over the thing that is besetting them, until their issues are resolved. Once issues are resolved, then the heart finds peace and rest.

Sometimes, people who were abandoned or suffered trauma as children, do things like decide in their mind to never have children so that they don't do what their biological parents did to them or they decide to have children out of wedlock to prove one can have a child and keep that child through thick and thin and thus prove their parents wrong. Or if their parents were divorced, they might decide to live with their significant other, because if they never marry, then they will never divorce and never do to their children what their parents did to them.

The goal for people struggling with these types of issues is to move to a more emotionally beneficial place. The goal is to resolve these issues, and to not be stuck but to live in freedom. The goal is to be motivated by *what is best for you* instead of *in response to what your parents did to you*. This is a better way to go through life.

The goal of moving on from one's past and into one's future is like the passing of a baton. When athletes pass the baton, for a little while the first athlete holds the baton by himself, then both athletes hold the baton at the same time, and then finally the first athlete lets the baton go and only the second athlete holds the baton by himself.

The emotional growth of one who was placed for adoption or into foster care (or who suffered any significant childhood trauma) can be similar to the passing of the baton between athletes. For one who is hurting from childhood pain, the first step to move forward is to gain insight that moving ahead, passing the baton is a good thing. The person must desire to pass the baton knowing that "freedom from the baton" lies ahead. More *freedom will be yours if you are able to let go of the "baton of your past"*. Freedom is your motivation. Your motive, is not to *respond to your parents*, your motive is to be *freed up on the inside*. Do you want freedom?

For one who is hurting from childhood pain, the *second step* to move forward as he gains desire to move ahead, he must like the two athletes, *hold both sides of the baton*. He must hold both the idea of *being uncomfortable with what happened to him at the same time as holding that acceptance of what happened to him can be useful for growth and maturity.*

Placing a child for adoption or into foster care is not God's best. Having suffered significant trauma as a child is not God's best. God does not want bad things to happen to children. Having an intact biological family is the best way and the way God intended things to be, but that doesn't mean that good can't be achieved in a different situation. While as a society we understand some parents become overwhelmed by life and feel they have no other option except placing children into homes, or some parents die and their children must be placed into homes because they are worthy of being cared for, or some parents are overcome by evil and society has an obligation to enter into these situations to protect children who are precious and deserve protection, we still affirm that to be in this situation hurts. If you are in this situation I want to first affirm your loss. I am sorry for your loss. Second, I want to encourage you that this is not the way God intended things to be. Third, I want you to generate an attitude of compassionate mercy for those who were incapable of parenting you. It is always wise to listen first to the details of what happened to you and why, because listening prevents errors in judgment. We don't make excuses for people but we are able as we are fathered by the Lord, to accept the way things are, to be healed, and to develop hearts of compassion for those who have hurt us. Challenges of attachment and bonding are greater for those who are in these situations, and thus you should receive care in order for your heart to be healed. You are worthy of being cared for. Healing takes time. Give yourself time to face the reality of your particular situation.

While you "hold the sorrow of your loss" you can also "hold onto the Lord" and accept that the Lord is for you, and He was with you through the tragedies in your life. While it may be true that your biological parent placed you into alternate care, the truth is God has been with you through it all and you are one person He will never give up if you remain in Him. The upside is your suffering can drive you to the Lord. God has good things in store for you, He is for you if you remain in Him. Also, you may have been protected from evil by being taken out of an unsafe situation, such as living on the street or being subject to abuse. The upside is you can become compassionate and helpful to others who are hurting. The upside is you can learn the value of hurtful, evil things to avoid and not be a part of. The upside is you can benefit others.

Holding the baton at the same time, means you understand that being placed for adoption or into foster care (or any childhood trauma) was bad because you suffered loss; but it also can be utilized for good if you trust in the Lord for your losses, find friendship with the Lord, and learn to live unselfishly for others.

Finally, the third step is to *resolve the cycle* and not hold onto the past hurt anymore. Like the athlete you can *let go of the baton of your hurt*, and allow for, be open to new opportunities, new possibilities. You can move into the future with confidence. One time I got hit by a truck, an eighteen-wheeler, and I walked away with only a severe whiplash. I refused to sue the truck company though people encouraged me to do so, and I could have made money, but instead I didn't sue and I gave thanks to the Lord, because I walked away with my life intact. Give thanks, glorify the Lord, *you have life left in you, you can rise up, you can overcome and you can be a light for others*. Use your suffering to help others, utilize your life to glorify the Lord and you will have reward in heaven. In weakness, His power is seen. Weakly depend on the Lord. Trust Him with your pain, He is trustworthy and He will bless you with His presence and with peace. I testify to you, He has done this for me.

Special Thanks To Jennifer Ann Canillas Fisher

Further Reading: Genesis 50:20, Romans 8:28-39

Have Fun!
The Big Picture

> *You who are young, be happy while you are young, and let your heart give you joy in the days of your youth. Follow the ways of your heart and whatever your eyes see, but know that for all these things God will bring you into judgment. Eccl 11:9*
>
> *How happy your people must be! How happy your officials, who continually stand before you and hear your wisdom! 1Kings 10:8*

The beautiful thing about God is that He brings purpose to our days. As God brings purpose and as we enter into that purpose our hearts find true happiness. The author of Ecclesiastes says simply to let your heart bring you happiness. The challenge for young people is to be certain that the correct things are making you happy, because God is not against joy and happy times,

He is against finding joy and happiness outside of Him. When God is put rightly in our lives in first place, then we begin to have the capacity to enjoy all things.

Proverbs says that laughter is a good medicine. God is the wellspring of joy and He is not opposed to happiness. If you are struggling with excessive sorrow, then get some help. Start filling your mind with cheerful things. Read some joke books and watch funny shows. One of my favorite shows on television in the 1990's was Home Improvement. Tim Allen always made me laugh with his goofy antics. Tim liked tools and sports and joking around. There are funny wholesome movies and funny wholesome series, it just sometimes takes work and effort to find the best ones. Funny Christian comics, Christian joke books and Christian comedians can all fuel our happiness. Many of these have made our family chuckle for hours. Finding and nurturing a culture of happiness is something worth working at. Hanging around Christians who are naturally cheery is also helpful. Some days we get totally wacky at our house with excessive rhymes and making up puns. Giving thanks and focusing your mind on the good things is an exercise of the mind that can be cultivated with care.

Further Study: Gen 30:13, 1 Kings 4:20, Ps 68:3, Ps 113:9, Prov 15:13, Prov 17:22, Eccl 3:12,5:19, 7:14; Zec 8:19, Mark 13:44, Matt 28:8, Luke 1:18, Luke 1:58, Luke 2:10, Luke 6:21-23, Acts 2:28, 2 Cor 7:9-13, Romans 14:17, James 5:13

Utilizing Echoes From Heaven For Group Study

All Lead: In order to make disciples, it is of utmost importance that everyone in the group understands that they can do the works of the Lord. The works of God is a privilege afforded to every believer and not only to those who are employed in paid ministerial positions. Therefore each person in the group should take turns in facilitating the discussion, purposely refraining from one strong leader being developed, and allowing every person to be developed as disciple makers side by side.

Study Focus: Decide as a group your desired area of focus. For example you could choose to do a twelve-week study on God or an eight-week study on suffering or a three-week study on unseen forces. You could choose to do a seven-week study on sins of the heart and pick the seven topics your group wants to focus on. You are free to adapt the material to meet your group's needs. Don't make unrealistic goals about studying all of the topics.

Administration: Once you have decided on your area of focus, assign leaders for the weeks you will meet. Leaders should attempt to read most or all of the supplemental study material at the end of the lesson, but others in the group also should be encouraged to do the supplemental reading if they have time. The idea is that the leader should come with an enriched understanding as leader for the week. The leader also should be in prayer for the people in the group.

Format: Discipleship Through Group Study

1. Open the session with praise and thanksgiving for God. Save prayers for supplication and confession for at the end of the study time. Focus in your prayers who you know God to be. God is creator. God is a covenantal God. God forgives. The members of the group should grow in their ability to verbalize simple praise about the character of God. One or two lines of praise per person is a good start. If it is helpful, the leader for the week might choose a psalm of praise for the group and ask the group members to praise in prayer from the Psalms. Recommended psalms include: psalm 8, 9, 11, 16, 18, 19, 21, 23, 29, 33, 34, 36, 46, 47, 48, 50, 63, 65, 66, 67, 68, 72, 75, 76, 84, 85, 89, 91, 92, 93, 95-100, 103-106, 108, 111-113, 116-118, 124, 135, 136, 138, 139, 144, 145, 146, 147, 149, and 150.

2. Read the Scriptures at the top of the devotional out loud. The leader should ask the group, "What truth or truths did this verse teach?" The leader should ask the group, "What truth or truths did the devotional being studied teach?"

3. The leader should then present what s/he has decided as the outstanding important supplementary passages to look up and discover together as a group. The leader then says, "Read this passage out loud." The leader then asks, "What did you get out of the passage? What do you think the passage is teaching?"

4. The leader may also prepare several simple open-ended questions to facilitate questions about the week's topic.

5. Leader asks, "How can you apply the truth of the devotional and the Scriptures to your life?"

6. Close in prayer. Remember ACTS. A=Adoration, C=Confession, T=Thanksgiving, S=Supplication (requests)

Understanding Christianity

In the book of Genesis, we learn that God made man and woman and he placed them in the Garden of Eden. Everything was perfect in the Garden of Eden. There was no pain or suffering. There are two places in the Bible where there is no suffering, the Garden of Eden in the book of Genesis and when Christ returns in the book of Revelations. But back to the Garden, it is here that we find that the serpent encouraged Eve to eat from the Tree of the Knowledge of Good and Evil, and yes, she did eat from it. After she ate from the Tree of the Knowledge of Good and Evil, she shared it with Adam and they both were cast out of the Garden of Eden. God told Adam and Eve not to eat from that Tree because if they did they would die. On that day, they fell into sin and the world has never been the same since.

The Old Testament is the history of God's people. After man fell into sin, men and women were in a state of being out of relationship with God and that is what sin means-it simply means to be separated from God. During this time of history, God's people are trained to give blood sacrifices to cover their sin so that they can be in relationship with God. Blood sacrifices were a temporary fix for sin. All throughout the Old Testament God's people were looking for the Messiah to come and be the one who would be the permanent one who would bridge the gap that had formed as a result of sin between God and man. So it went on like this for hundreds of years with blood sacrifices being offered for temporary atonement of sin, but no permanent solution to sin, no Messiah had come yet. This is the history that is recorded in the Old Testament.

And then everything changed. Jesus was born. Jesus is the permanent solution to the problem of sin. Jesus is the one who bridges the gap- the breach- between man and God. In the New Testament there are four Gospels. These Gospels are a record of the history of Jesus' life on earth. Now I will tell you, that people today still disagree about whether or not Jesus is the Messiah, but no thinking educated person does not believe Jesus lived. Jesus undeniably lived. Jesus' life on earth was so remarkable that since he lived we started counting years forward. Up until the time of Jesus time is referred to as B.C., meaning before Christ. 100 years BC meant 100 years before Jesus was born. 200 B.C. means 200 years before Christ et cetera. Now, the year that I am publishing this book is 2016 A.D. It has been 2016 years since Jesus lived on the earth. You see my friend, you cannot be an agnostic, a Hindu, a Buddhist, a Jew, a Muslim or an atheist and have any integrity and deny the reality that Jesus Christ lived and died. It is not disputable. Jesus lived and died. Now you may disagree with his identity of who he said he was, but you simply cannot deny that he lived. Jesus was so unique that the calendar changed after his presence on the earth.

Dear friend, I proclaim to you that Jesus is the Messiah that the Jews were searching for all along. He fit the criteria; he fulfilled the multitude of prophecies that are woven throughout all of the Old Testament. Jesus paid the costly price of being rejected, and crucified to be the final atonement for sin-your sin and my sin. I believe he is the Messiah. But don't take my word for it, find out for yourself. He can and he will reveal himself to you if you search for God with all your heart, you will find him to be real. Don't miss him, friend, don't miss him. So, the Gospels tell the great story of Jesus. Matthew, Mark, Luke, and John were four men who each wrote down an account of the life of Jesus. With Jesus' life, ministry, death and resurrection, the New Testament church was born.

The second great story of the New Testament is that Gentiles, who formerly were not a part of the community of faith, now were grafted into the body of believers. The book immediately following the Gospels is the Acts of the Apostles. The Book of Acts tells the story of the early church as the church is empowered with the Holy Spirit. Other books in the New Testament explain how Jews and Gentiles became united as Christians together and the struggles they encountered to become a unified people of faith, as well as letters to early churches.

Additionally, the New Testament also has a third great story, which is in the last book of the Bible, the Book of Revelation. Revelation records the future, yet to come. Herein lies the great hope of all Christians, the return of Jesus Christ to rule the earth and to eventually make all things new.

How To Become a Christian

If you have never heard, it is very simple. It is simply Jesus. It is Jesus simply Jesus. Do you want Jesus? Jesus wants you, but the question remains, do you want Him? You don't have to know everything, you don't have to understand everything, what you must do is cry out to Him, welcome Him into your heart, and ask Him to be your Savior. Scripture says in John 1:12, yet to all who did receive him, to those who believed in his name, he gave the right to become children of God. He loves and embraces all who humble themselves and come to him. The important thing here is to know that Jesus is God's provision for you, he is your covering, and He is your life raft. You are getting into Jesus' boat. You can trust him as the Messiah who carried your sins, took your shame and suffered for you. He is your atonement.

Atonement is a big word but it simply means He is the provision made by God to cleanse you from your sin. In the Old Testament the Jews covered their doorposts with the blood of the lamb and the angel of death passed over them and their firstborn were saved because they trusted in the Lord's provision and protection and hence their children were not killed while the firstborn Egyptians perished. Jesus is your protection. When you choose Jesus, you are choosing God's way, though you might not understand everything, you do understand that Jesus said, "I am the Way, the Truth, and the Life. No man comes to the Father but by me." God said that Jesus is the only way to God. Jesus is the Lamb of God provided to take away the sins of

203

the world. Jesus is the Lamb of God who died on the cross for your sins, so that you can have a fresh start. So, Jesus, then is the one, he is the one who has permanently bridged the gap between God and man.

It is important to realize that Jesus said, "You must be born again to enter the kingdom of heaven." Jesus also said, "For God so loved the world that he gave his only begotten son, that whosoever believes in him would not perish but have everlasting life, for as many as received him, to them he gave power to become children of God." Entering God's family does not take a seminary degree. Entering God's family does not take following a system of church rules or moral rules. Entering God's family does not happen by being good enough. No! Entering God's family takes a heart of belief and a heart that welcomes the Messiah, Jesus into one's heart. Jesus is the atoning sacrifice for our sins. But what does that mean? In the Old Testament God required a blood sacrifice for sin, but now, God has provided THEE FINAL SACRIFICE, JESUS. Jesus took our place on the cross, the penalty we deserved because we choose to live outside of God and that choice is sin. The most important command is to love God with all of our heart, mind, and soul; and the truth is we have not passionately pursued God. We have sinned and fallen short. And the payment for that sin is death-both physical death and spiritual death. We are separated from God because of our sin. But God in his kindness has provided a way out. God in his kindness came to earth, took our place on the cross, took our punishment, he suffered, died and was buried and on the third day he rose from the grave. And he became sin for us in order that we might find life in God. God gave us this costly gift, but nonetheless for us it is a free gift, all we have to do is receive the gift, accept the gift, it is ours. Believe on the Lord Jesus Christ and you will be saved. If you declare with your mouth that Jesus is Lord and believe in your heart that God raised him from the dead, you will be saved.

If you are ready to receive Jesus as your personal Savior then you can do it at this very moment. You can ask Jesus into your heart by praying this simple prayer. Lord Jesus, I confess I am a sinner, and you Jesus are Lord. I believe in my heart that God raised you Jesus, from the dead for my atonement. I receive you as my Savior. I put my trust in you now. Please forgive my sins and help me to follow you.

If you have prayed that prayer make sure you tell someone that you have received Jesus into your heart.

Endnotes

"Smith's Bible Dictionary." Blue Letter Bible. Web. 06 Apr. 2016.

Musixmatch. *AZlyrics.com*. Web.13 Apr. 2016. King and Country lyrics-Busted Heart.

"Aristotle, Metaphysica Quotes," *Quotes.net*. STANDS4 LLC, 2016. 13 April 2016. http://www.quotes.net/quote/38481.

.

www.ingramcontent.com/pod-product-compliance
Lightning Source LLC
Chambersburg PA
CBHW070350090426
42733CB00009B/1360